THERE'S ALWAYS SOMETHING YOU CAN DO

Women's Engaging Stories and your Financial Future

By Heather Duncan, CFP

Enjoy!

> "I am only one, but still I am one.
> I cannot do everything, but still I can do something.
> I will not refuse to do the something I can do."
>
> Helen Keller 1880 - 1968

Heather Duncan

There's Always Something You Can Do:
Women's Engaging Stories and Your Financial Future

By Heather Duncan, CFP

Copyright © 2003, Heather Duncan, CFP

Published by Book Coach Press
Canadian Office: Ottawa, Ontario
United States Office: Danville, California

www.BookCoachPress.com

Heather Duncan, CFP
P.O. Box 4704, Station "E"
Ottawa, ON   K1S 5H8
Canada

www.heatherduncan.ca
(613) 236-1733
1-866-821-0233

National Library of Canada Cataloguing in Publication

Duncan, Heather, 1960-
    There's Always Something You Can Do:
    Women's Engaging Stories and Your Financial Future

ISBN 0-9680347-7-2

    1. Women--Finance, Personal. 2. Financial security. I. Title.

HG179.D845 2003   332.024'042   C2003-905160-9

Production Credits
Book cover design: Nation Media & Design
Printing: The Tri-Co Group Inc. (Printed on recycled paper)

Dedicated to
the late

Phyllis Hastings McKim

&

Sarah Anne Duncan

I think of you and miss you
Every single day

Acknowledgements

What an amazing experience it is to write a book. At first, when the idea of what you want to say strikes you like lightning, you are immediately energized and your step is full of spring. Inspiration has given you a mission, a new outlook on life and a new identity. Now you are a would-be author. You want to contribute to the world, you want those who know you to be proud of you, you want to do your best.

But the euphoric, all-powerful stage doesn't last long, and that's a very good thing. Now your journey becomes filled with questions and you are forced not only to accept the responsibility of your dream, but to be honest with yourself. Writing a book which is designed to share advice with others calls for some self-examination. In the process, you slowly become aware of your strengths, but you quickly become aware of your weaknesses. As you continue to write, you still hope that your book will inspire others, but you realize that the person who needed to hear your message most, was you.

I am so glad I took this journey. And don't we meet the most wonderful people when we're travelling? First and foremost, I want to thank the remarkable women who share their stories in *There's Always Something You Can Do*. They've put their intelligence, senses of humour and hearts out on their sleeves. I think you will come to respect and appreciate them as much as I do. They have shared their experiences freely and openly for the benefit of others. How can you not admire them? Thank you, ladies.

In the process of writing this book I had two coaches. Serena Williamson Andrew was my "book coach" and Dorothy Kate MacDonald was my Jin Shin Do specialist and "life coach." I couldn't have completed this project without either of you. You were my bookends (pardon the pun) – you helped me stand straight on the shelf and acted as buttresses when I thought I was tipping over.

There are women who have come before me, writing in the field of financial planning. They have unknowingly been my mentors. I say unknowingly, because even though I've read their work for many years, and I have been impressed by their knowledge, integrity and facility for communication, I've never met them in person. To Ellen Roseman, Joanne Thomas Yaccato and Gail Vaz-Oxlade, I want to say thank you for setting the bar so high. I am a huge fan and I have been for a long time. You have made a difference in peoples' lives.

My clients also deserve a big thank you. Most of them did not know I was attempting to write a book while carrying a full workload during a three year bear market. Of course I tried to hide my distraction and frazzlement, but I'm sure it was often visible. I've said many times that I have the nicest clients – they are kind, understanding, patient and funny. Thank you for being delightful to work with.

To my assistant, Dianne, and the men at Nation Media & Design, who let me share their space, including "Snappy" the turtle – you keep me on my toes and make me laugh.

To my Mom, my immediate family and my great friends – gosh you know who you are because I love you so dearly. Thank you for your never-ending support. Life asks us to make so many decisions. I can move forward because you are standing behind me. You are my riches. And to the next generation: Gloria, Taylor, Vanessa, MacKenna, Emmett, and my goddaughter Anna, I stand behind you all the way. "Auntie Heather" is perhaps your biggest cheerleader. I look forward to every thing you will do. You will each make the world a more beautiful place.

To my husband Marc, who never had one ounce of doubt that I could write a book. Marc, you tell me you love me every day and nothing beats that – it's a great feeling. Your optimism is contagious, everybody says so and they are right. Thank you for having no doubts!

PS: And a very special thank you to the printer of this book, my sister, the one and only Lisa Duncan. There's nothing that woman can't do.

Table of Contents

Chapter One

The Lay of the Land

At the early stages of writing, a friend and mentor asked me if this was a book about taking control. It's not. I've had enough life experience and enough professional experience to appreciate how little we control. Our individual life span is an incredible journey. Not only is it unplanned - who asked to be born - but once you are on the journey, so much of your time is spent figuring out the lay of the land. We are given no map or detailed directions, and sometimes very little guidance. I'm 41 but I still feel like I'm 21 and it makes me appreciate how little my parents knew when they were my age. We learn a lot through trial and error.

This book is about preparing and planning, not about being in control financially all the time. Preparing considers the big picture, the overview, and addresses issues that are universal to us all. Planning includes the more individual scenario; adapted and updated with our personal, changing circumstances. Preparing involves reflection and thought, while planning leads to action and adaptation. Preparation is more philosophical. Planning is practical. *There's Always Something You Can Do* addresses both aspects.

It would seem that a book which ponders the meaning of financial planning is an odd slant on a well-known, overly-advertised, media-friendly, lifestyle topic. But the truth is that in the madness of living we have lost sight of why we need to do financial planning and what it actually is. In some ways we've made it a more complicated topic than it needs to be, and we've become paralyzed or paranoid in the process. It reminds me of two other areas of our lives: exercise and nutrition.

Not that many years ago, how many people had to give thought to getting enough exercise and eating right? Children walked to and from school, and even if they didn't live on a farm there were chores to do, which we would now consider manual labour. Men weren't sitting in traffic for an hour's commute to work, only to be chained to their computers for 10 hours once they got there. Women worked in a home where there were no disposable diapers, no microwave ovens, no ready-made anything. Not only did they have the responsibility of running the home, but women also worked on the farm, in factories and offices too. And there was laundry to do – you didn't drop off your clothes at the drycleaners – everything was washed, ironed and mended by hand.

And eating right? Well the first thing you ate was anything you could grow in your garden, or bake in your home. You bought locally. No one had "smart" fridges or chest freezers. You certainly didn't have to read labels to avoid food with additives/preservatives/chemicals you couldn't pronounce. You didn't have to worry about how much junk food you consumed because there wasn't any.

And did anyone count grams of carbohydrates to make sure they stayed within the zone? Did anyone worry about portion control a hundred years ago? There was no "biggie" this and "jumbo size" that. In fact, if you have tea or coffee cups you have inherited from a couple of generations back, compare them in size to the mugs in your home now. For fun, imagine how many tea cups it would take to fill the largest sized serving at your local coffee shop or the largest soft-drink container from the nearest fast food outlet.

Of course exercise and nutrition are multi-billion dollar industries today. A hundred years ago there wasn't much need for personal trainers or weight loss clinics. But to maintain a healthy life within our crazy 24/7 lifestyles we rely on many professionals including certified trainers and qualified nutritionists. Well it's a similar story when it comes to financial planning, but for a very different reason: we are living longer.

At the beginning of the 20th century you had a good life if you lived into your 50's. Today, you would love to be retired by the time you reach your 50's and you are certainly not getting ready to die. In fact a new life is beginning. Your retirement years could now be longer than your working life and that's what we want to plan for. It's not just the first 15 years in retirement which is our concern. More importantly it is the second 15 years when our health is declining and we may be on our own without a partner. Or we've found that we have become the aging caregiver to an aging spouse. I recently became aware of two women who are 106, one in my own family. She is my paternal grandmother's sister-in-law who lives in England. I haven't met her but I understand she relies heavily on her son who must be in his mid-seventies, at least. As time goes on, this family situation will become more and more common. A client pointed out that no longer are we a part of the sandwich generation, it's now the club sandwich generation.

> **"Age is strictly a case of mind over matter. If you don't mind it doesn't matter."**
> Jack Benny, American comedian

As a Certified Financial Planner there is so much I want to share with you. Sometimes people feel badly when they meet with me, as though they feel guilty because they can no longer manage their investments, or they don't know where to start. I reassure them: there is a reason my job exists. It's a lot more complicated in the investment, taxation and insurance worlds than it used to be. We are inundated with information through the media and by advertising from the financial services industry. Everybody wants a piece of your pie. We either don't know where to begin, or we don't know where to go for trustworthy advice.

Here are my goals for *There's Always Something You Can Do*: That you will find the book to be refreshing, enlightening and inspiring. That you will be reassured that you can do financial planning; you will know what you need to do and why. That you'll like taking responsibility for your well being, and you will appreciate how nobody gets it right 100% of the time. We have all made mistakes, but you will discover that financial planning is actually fun because it is empowering. As you read further, you may see yourself in some of the stories told here. In fact, I hope you will feel so inspired you'll want to tell every 20-something how important it is to be self-sufficient so they can be happy, healthy and productive into their 80's and beyond.

This book will help you to appreciate how amazingly blessed we are to live in the time that we do. With our options come responsibilities, but they're worth it. If we take care of ourselves and our planet each of us can have rewarding lives with a lot less worry. And, you will realize that as result of our lengthening life spans, newspapers are going to have to make room for longer and longer obituaries because we are learning, growing and accomplishing more and more. Are lives are becoming longer and fuller.

The decision to write these pages resulted from my professional experience and my personal passion. I hope everyone will find this book accessible and informative, but I want to be honest and tell you that my overriding concern is for women. Women make up 51% of the population in Canada, and on average women still outlive men by at least 10 years in North America. Remember, those are the last 10 years when we are most frail and most vulnerable. This is not a book of statistics. I don't want to knock you over the head with all kinds of data supporting the plight of aging women and the numbers of them who are dependent or falling under the poverty line. Certainly there are many elderly men living in poverty too. But as we look around, we recognize that each of us, regardless of our gender, is aging every single day and "... there but for the grace of God go I."

There's Always Something You Can Do is dedicated to my grandmothers. Phyllis was born in 1898 in England and died in 1990. Sarah was born in 1900 in Scotland and died in 1995. Both of them emigrated to Canada in the 1920's, married and had families. They lived into their nineties. They lived through two world wars and the great depression, plus many other political upheavals and economic crises. Their lives covered the period from the horse & buggy to rockets, moon walks and space shuttles. The whole history of flight developed in their lifetime. These women also spent a great portion of their lives in widowhood. Phyllis was widowed for almost 60 years. She was the wife of an Anglican minister and was left with three children under the age of 6. Sarah was widowed for over 30 years with no pension from her husband's company nor any Canada Pension Plan benefits (CPP only started in 1967). At the end of my life, I'd like to think I will answer to them. I know they would want me to advise other women on the realities of living into old age. And who knows, maybe one day I will get to see them again and after getting the best hugs they will say "Heather we're so proud of you."

If as a result of reading this book you establish your financial goals and review them regularly; you figure out your personal living expenses and how to live beneath them; you calculate your uncommitted monthly income and allocate it proportionately toward your goals; you make a commitment to your financial security and feed your retirement savings plan; you purchase a life insurance, critical illness and/or long term care policy; and you have your will and powers of attorney updated, then I will have done my job and my grandmothers will be smiling.

We are so lucky to be alive right now. Yes, we are overwhelmed with options and stressed-out by the expectations placed on us. We have a daily love/hate relationship with the clock, the traffic, our email, and the supersaturation of information. But our grandmothers and great-grandmothers either dreamed of these opportunities or fought for them. Phyllis' family in England thought she was crazy to move to the prairies of Canada in the first place, but once she was widowed they thought for sure she would come to her senses and return to England. She didn't. It was important to her to raise her children in this country. She moved to a fishing village in Ontario where she could afford to purchase a small house, giving her a bit of land to grow the vegetables that would feed her children daily. Apparently she wasn't a great cook, but she sure could garden.

Many years later a small inheritance from a brother-in-law allowed her to retire in dignity. What did that mean to Phyllis? It meant volunteering with the Save the Children Fund and sponsoring girls in other countries as foster children. Not only would she correspond with these young women, she would visit them. Children around the world were real to her, and there was nothing she was more proud of than the education her children, grandchildren and foster children achieved. Phyllis was ahead of her time in many ways, but she was no more in control of her life than you or I.

Sarah was number five of ten children so she was pulled out of school after grade 9 to stay at home and help with the housework as well as looking after her younger siblings. Helping with the housework in 1915 meant cleaning out coal fireplaces, polishing brass, doing the laundry (no automatic washer or dryer), peeling the vegetables (no pre-washed, cut veggies in plastic bags at the supermarket, in fact no supermarket). Sarah always regretted her limited education and she had a unique curiosity throughout her life. Her favourite book was the atlas and her favourite TV show in her late eighties was Jeopardy. You knew not to phone Sarah if Jeopardy was on TV. She retired on the grocery money she had saved over many, many years. It didn't last. She spent the last five years of her life financially dependent on the government and the assistance of her daughter-in-law and grandchildren.

Throughout the book you will hear the voices and stories of other women. These are not compilations, these are real people. I approached individuals and asked them if they would help me reach others through their experiences. These are wonderful women of different ages and backgrounds. Some can relax because they are financially confident, others do not feel so secure. All of them believe as I do that financial planning should not be a taboo subject, and that women especially need to plan and look out for themselves early on. Life comes with no guarantees.

In my practice I work with people from age 18 up. I love the diversity of my practice, from young families who are starting education plans for their small children to the widowed who are extremely grateful for insurance proceeds and the chance to stay in their homes. But often when driving back at night from an appointment, it would strike me that while I get to see the whole spectrum of life's stages through my clients, individually some of them had limited experience or a very narrow perspective. I felt I was more concerned about their financial well being than they were – or realized they should be. Because of confidentiality, I couldn't reveal other client's experiences or how others had been affected in certain situations. And I realized what I really wanted was to have some of my older clients sit down with some of my younger clients to share the lessons they had learned, to give them the lay of the land.

I hope this book will fulfill that dream. When I first started working as a financial planner, my manager used to call me Florence Nightingale because I wanted to go out and heal everybody, and it's true. But like you, I've quickly come to realize there are only 24 hours in the day and I am only one person. So with the inspiration of Helen Keller: "I will not refuse to do the something I can do" and through the support and generosity of the wonderful people who share their wisdom on these pages, you and I can work together to improve our chances of enjoying a productive life, a comfortable retirement and a dignified old age.

> **"A single gentle rain makes the grass many shades greener. So our prospects brighten on the influx of better thoughts. We should be blessed if we lived in the present always, and took advantage of every accident that befell us."**
>
> Henry David Thoreau, *Walden*

Chapter Two

Razia S.

Razia is 31 and married. She and her husband Chris are the parents of a one year old daughter, Arianna

How old were you when you found out you had Multiple Sclerosis?

I was twenty years old when I was first diagnosed. I had started having problems prior to that but my actual diagnosis was at 20 years of age. It was a difficult diagnosis to receive but it made me more conscious that I'm not going to let tomorrow just happen. I'm going to plan for tomorrow but I'm not going to live for tomorrow. I decided to live for today.

It's today that's important. Tomorrow, I don't know what will occur and I think my mother's death influenced that. She died back in 1995 when she was 51 years old. She was in a car accident and it was totally, totally unexpected. My father and mother had so many plans for their retirement together. I want to make sure that if I do get to the "when we retire" stage I'm OK, but it's now that's important.

And my daughter, she's the main priority in my life. Nothing else compares to her. She's a joy, she's such a joy. I want to make sure that she is set and that she learns how to take care of herself. If anything ever happened to Chris, God forbid, I would survive. I know I would do anything to survive. But if I go and Chris goes, we want our daughter to be protected and that's the reason we're doing financial planning now. Before our purpose wasn't that but now that we have her, it has changed our focus in every area, not just financial planning. Waking up in the morning, it's vital for me to make sure I'm ready for her. To start the day with her and to put her to bed at night, that's one of my biggest joys.

You have lived with MS for ten years now and it hasn't slowed you down.

I won't let it slow me down but that's my attitude. Some people aren't like that. My attitude is OK, I have this disease and yeah, its bad and there are definitely difficult times, but I'm not going to let it stop me from doing what I want to do. Especially now with Arianna, I don't want to stop going out and doing things with her because of my MS which is one of the reasons I started the medication I am taking. The needles, oh I hate taking those needles, I detest them. Mixing them and stabbing myself, you know the whole thing. The medication is so expensive, which is one of the reasons I went back to work after my daughter was born. I want to be able to function for as long as possible and this medication is supposed to help in the long run. So I will do whatever I can and that includes going back to work. I'm thankful I have a really good health plan through my employer. My salary doesn't matter, that's how grateful I am to have a benefit plan which allows me to take this medicine. I sympathize with those that can't afford it.

What makes you normal or average is to be married with your first child at the age of thirty-one, a home, a mortgage and a dog. But your planning must be a little bit different. Could you live to be ninety with MS?

Oh I could. There is no time limit with MS. I am functional. I'm good now. I don't know how I am going to be in ten years, there could be different complications. But don't forget, since I was diagnosed ten years ago they have come up with the medication I'm now taking. They've come up with three or four different medications in that time. I only started on medicine this year, so I was basically nine years without. All the damage that was done in those nine years, I might not see now, but I could see ten years from now.

I want to make sure I am prepared so that if I need help, if I need extra medical attention, if I need a wheelchair, if I need to get a house that's accessible to a wheelchair, I can. That's why we are doing financial planning. And for Arianna too. We looked at setting up her RESP even before she was born so she could have everything she needed by the time she goes to university.

You are my only client where we had the RESP application opened before the baby was born, before she had a social insurance number, before she had a birth certificate. You and Chris have been good about living within your means.

No we haven't!

OK, that won't go in the book.

No, we've lived beyond our means but we've done important stuff. We're taking care of our RRSPs, that's important to us. We're paying our mortgage which is important. To me, as long as I have a roof over my head, food on the table, and love in this house, I'm doing OK.

Recently we put my grandmother in a nursing home and I went to visit her there and it was terrible, terrible. And you know what? I don't want to have to be in there, in that circumstance. There's no way I want to be in that situation. My heart just breaks, it's not right but there was nothing we could do as a family, nobody could take care of her. I hate the fact that she is in there. I wish we could have afforded something better for her.

My grandmothers weren't able to remain in their own homes either, so I know exactly how you are feeling. Razia, you have life insurance which if we tried to get now, I'm not sure we would be able to. How did you come to have life insurance so early?

At the time I was diagnosed I was working for an advertising agency. The owner's brother was in the insurance business and that's when I got life insurance. They knew I had MS so I guess the criteria were not as tough back then, and I was very young. Because of the MS we opted to get a whole life policy instead of term insurance.

Tell me, what did you learn about finances from your family?

My mom taught me how to be frugal that's for sure. I love shopping cheap. I love buying $5 shoes and a suit for $25. And my dad taught me to manage my money. I was really bad early on, when I first moved out at 17. Looking back I thought I knew everything at 17. It would be good if I could go back then with the knowledge I have now. Not that I know everything now!

So financially, being away from home and on your own at university, you must have learned some things the hard way.

Oh yeah, I was very, very bad. I was totally, completely up to my ears in debt. My mother kept bailing me out and I kept getting myself back in debt, and then my mother kept bailing me out again. And then I met Chris who used to have his cheques balanced to the penny. I learned some things from him, but now he's changed completely. He doesn't really care about day-to-day finances any more and I've taken over the responsibility of the bills and managing our accounts. We've been gearing towards retirement and making sure that Arianna has the opportunity to have the education she wants. I'm not going to force her but I want her to try. I think she will. Probably every parent feels the same. And I'm glad I have life insurance. If anything happens to me, Chris can pay off the debts.

When your mom passed away, did that change things financially for you? Did you look at things differently?

The biggest thing that changed was my outlook: what's going to happen in the future is going to happen. I can't know so I'm going to live for today, not for then. But, that doesn't mean I'm not going to prepare. And that's when I started living within my means. I was lucky, I had started my RSP but only because of Chris. He was more financially sound then.

It's funny how those roles reverse.

Oh yeah. I think it's totally weird that I'm the one managing the money now because I was so bad at it and he was so good. But I don't mind.

And did your mom have some life insurance through her work when she passed away?

She had everything. Both my parents were insured to the max. My brother was travelling when she died and he was able to come home from London on the Concorde because everything was paid for.

That's why the money is there. It's to help however it is needed. It's not to make anyone a multi-millionaire.

Exactly and that's something my father taught me too. There are also some wonderful things that, when I look back, I know my mom taught me and I'm thankful for. I'm hoping I'm a good mother, and if I am it comes from her. If I could be one millionth of the person she was, I would be ecstatic.

What do you want Arianna to know financially? What do you want to teach your daughter?

Independence, to be financially secure. I think that's my biggest fear, not being able to take care of myself. My grandmother's in a nursing home in her eighties and my mom died too soon in her fifties. I look at life now and everything happens for a reason. It made me grow up. I thought I was grown up. I want Arianna to learn. I know there are going to be times when she will say to me "Yeah, yeah Mom, what do you know?" I know those times will happen. But if I can put it in her mind that she's got to prepare, that she's got to take care of herself, then eventually she'll come around, because that's what my mother did for me.

One thing I'm hoping that women will learn from this book is that it doesn't matter how old you are, at the earliest time that you can, get life insurance. That's important. Start your financial planning now, at the earliest moment you are able to. For Arianna we did it before she was born by setting up her education plan. I want women to start thinking, because something could happen to them the way it happened to me.

And not enough young women have life insurance.

Yes, it's important. Not everybody is partnered up with somebody but you're going to be eventually. If there's any care of children or any future that you want to protect, you want to do it now in case something happens later on.

First of all, let me tell you how I was diagnosed. I used to read and study a lot and I noticed a grey area, a blocked out area in one of my eyes. I thought I'll go and get it checked and I went to my family doctor. He looked at my eyes and identified the area saying it would probably clear itself up. He said "worse case scenario: MS, so we'll just do a little added test to rule that out." I said OK, fine. Then I started to have test after test. I had EKGs, then an MRI, then a CAT scan. It was basically six months to a year of tests. I was diagnosed through my eyesight, just that one grey line. That one grey line was vital.

MS is very uncommon not only in my family background, but in my heritage. You are seeing more and more diagnoses of MS now and they still don't know why one person gets it over another. It's yucky to take the needles I take every week and it hurts. I was taking huge needles at the beginning until I learned that I could get much smaller ones. And me, with no fat. I'm thinner than I've ever been in my life. I try not to think about MS, I figure that if I don't dwell on it, maybe it'll disappear.

You can't dwell on it because you are too busy being a mom, a wife, an employee, a friend, a sister, a sister-in-law, a daughter, and all the other roles you play.

But you know what? I love every single role and I hope that I am doing a good job. I pray that I am and that people will learn from me through this book, and someone who reads it will say, "Wow, maybe I should get my health checked now, maybe I should start planning now." Financially plan for your future. You are worth this. Do the best planning that you can and then take life one day at a time.

And be grateful for the ability to put your daughter to bed.

I give Arianna a kiss every night. She's one of the best things I've ever hoped for. Every day when I get home from work, I look forward to seeing her. I used to go out all the time and have my own life; do what I needed to do, when I wanted to do it, how I wanted to do it. And that's all changed. I like being a mother, I think I was meant to be a mother. And after six years of trying it just happened. We did the fertility thing. I was on fertility medication and then I said if I don't get pregnant naturally, then I don't get pregnant at all. I went off the medication but I had an invitro appointment and the week before I cancelled it too. I thought I am not going to play God; if it's meant to happen, it will. I had decided to focus on going back to school and doing what I could for myself.

I finished my schooling, got my Microsoft Systems Certified Engineer designation, and one month later I was pregnant. It was totally natural and totally unexpected. I remember when we found out we were all jumping outside screaming. Everybody in the neighbourhood heard because the weather was beautiful and people were outdoors. *Everyone* was jumping up and down.

There you go, Arianna was meant to happen. I hope that one day you will give her this book and she will be inspired to be financially self-sufficient. She will also know how much she was wanted and loved.

Chapter Three

Looking Back

> "The last of the human freedoms is to choose one's attitude in any given set of circumstances, to choose one's own way."
>
> Viktor Frankl, Holocaust survivor

How does that saying go? It's not what happens to you in life, it's how you handle it. Sometimes we feel we are limited in what we can do financially or what we can achieve financially, and we don't try to do anything beyond getting through another day. However "getting through another day" should not be underestimated if you are dealing with an illness, if you are physically hurt, in mental or emotional pain. Getting through that day is an achievement. If you have a sick child or an elderly parent who is in any way dependent on you, if you have a spouse who is away because of work, unhappy at work or concerned about his or her business, then you know how much those circumstances can deplete your energy. If you are unemployed or feeling trapped, you truly understand what an accomplishment it can be to get through another day with your sanity intact.

At the same time we need to remember that life won't always be the way we are experiencing it right now. We can make changes, small and large, even when we are overwhelmed. Of course when we want change to occur in our life it rarely happens at the speed we'd like, but that's okay. Our life spans have increased so much in the last century that the good news is we have lots of time to make many changes. We will experience and handle more than our great-grandparents ever dreamed of. So not only do we have more time to make mistakes, we have more time to recover from them too. Failure is a part of success. Without failure there would be no success; success would be a completely neutral term, neither here nor there. It would have no meaning, no value. I once read that experience is what you get when you don't get what you want.

Life is cumulative. It is not just today or the current situation in which we find ourselves that defines our life or our sense of success. It's absolutely true that some life-changes will not occur until we make a huge, sustained effort to turn things around: hard, difficult change that doesn't happen overnight. However, you also know or you've experienced the ability to make small changes, which have had a positive effect completely out of proportion to the action you have taken.

Have you ever gone from having no savings to setting up an automatic plan of $50 a month coming from your bank account and going into a separate savings or investment account? Now in your head you know you are not going to be able to retire on $50 a month, but how great did it feel to set up that plan? You took one small step for your own financial security, and one giant leap for your sense of empowerment and hope. If you don't dwell on the fact that you can't retire on your new savings plan, but instead focus on the fact that you got it started, you'll be self-inspired to increase it to $75 dollars monthly as soon as possible, and more after that. Just like a runner you have discovered there is a high in taking that first step by starting to save, and the ultimate high is knowing you're on the right track. You've begun to do some planning and you're better prepared for life financially than you were 24 hours ago.

Sometimes we get overwhelmed at the thought of financial planning because the gap between where we'd like to be financially and where we are seems like a chasm. As a result, we don't move into action but stay mired in the thought of what we really should be doing: paying ourselves first, putting more money into our retirement plan, eliminating consumer debt, reviewing our need for insurance in case of sickness or disability, and looking at life insurance, especially if we would leave dependents (children, parents, a spouse) behind. All those "shoulds" and "ifs" become overwhelming and rather than self-inspiring they can feel self-defeating.

A strategic coach by the name of Dan Sullivan addresses this stumbling block. He calls it "living in the gap." (I call it a chasm.) We want to avoid "living in the gap" although we need to be aware of when we're in it in order to pull ourselves out. Living in the gap means that our focus is on the expanse between our reality and our dreams. The gap never disappears, like a mirage it's always beyond our grasp. The mirage provides us with no permanent satisfaction. Rather, we need to encourage and motivate ourselves to keep moving forward by reflecting on how far we've already come. It sounds like heresy but it's true. Sometimes we need to spend less time looking forward, fixated on where we want to be, and spend a little more time looking back, appreciating the distance and geography we have already traveled.

This applies not only to financial planning, but to our overall happiness. Dan believes that happiness is a skill. It's not something that is given to us, it is something we choose. We create and develop happiness for ourselves. To do so we need to continually and quietly appreciate our achievements and review our journey.

> **"Achievement is always about effort, not about talent."**
>
> Jim Taylor, psychologist and author

We all have a vision in our mind's eye of our ideal life, the kind of life we'd like to be living, preferably right now. Some days that vision might be kind of murky, other days it is crystal clear. Of course at other times we're so preoccupied with getting through the day we forget that we are dreamers by our very nature. Visions, dreams, ideals are concepts which speak to our humanity, they are universal concepts. Each of us has the ability to dream. We live in the gap/chasm when the majority of our attention is focussed on how much we are **not** living the picture in our heads, as opposed to reflecting on our progress. We need to shine a spotlight on our own growth and development. Yes, we've learned lots along the way and we've made plenty of mistakes, but we have done many things right too.

The reason for having a vision of the ideal life, which would certainly include financial security if not financial independence, is that it inspires us. Your vision of the ideal provides the motivation you need to pursue your goals, and as Dan Sullivan points out, it allows us to withstand hardships. The ideal is a mental concept. It is your picture of the vision that is unique, and it could be very different from someone else's. For example, my mother lives in a log home on 17 acres, outside a small village that no one beyond a 30 kilometre radius has ever heard of. That lifestyle is a thousand times closer to my mom's vision of the ideal than it is to mine. But no one who knows my mom would deny how hard she has worked to pursue her dream of a cabin in the woods, and to live the life she has chosen. The ideal orients our compass. It's our northern star. What we experience is the journey of getting there – the blood, sweat, tears and joy of moving toward our dream. Hope keeps us going and it spurs us on to great accomplishments, big and small, public and private.

> **"People are trapped in history and history is trapped in them."**
> James Baldwin, American author

Have you ever taken a few minutes to reflect on what you learned about money as you were growing up? As part of preparing for tomorrow financially, I think it is important that we give some thought to what we absorbed, consciously or unconsciously, about money from our family and our extended families. One of the first things we discover is that everything has a price attached to it.

Of course as a very young child the price of something doesn't mean anything. If you saw a toy you wanted in a store or on a TV commercial and were told it was "too expensive," then all you heard, translated into a child's vocabulary, was, "You're not going to get it without a fight. Since I'm not saying yes, right away, then if you really want this you are going to have to come up with some other strategy to get me to agree." Too expensive is a relative concept and young children have no experience acquiring money or managing cash flow. Usually it wasn't until we had our own allowance or we'd been given some money to spend that we began to understand it didn't go far enough.

What we didn't learn by example in our families, we learned by absorption. If money was the source of horrible arguments between your parents, or one of the reasons you were raised in a single-parent home, you fully understood even at a young age how emotional the subject of money can be.

Maybe you were raised in a home where money was not a concern, but understanding, love and nurturing were scarce. Or the opposite, you were as poor as church mice but you had a sense of togetherness and security. Either way, if you take a few minutes to reflect you'll discover there is a lot you can learn from your background and family.

Maybe now that you are a "grown-up" you wonder how your parents or grandparents did it? Ask them. If you have older family members, friends or acquaintances you respect, and you approach them with respect, they will happily share their experiences, including what they did right and the mistakes they believe they made. They could have some useable ideas, or their situation may have been so different from your current life that their memories will allow you to further appreciate how the world has changed and how people adjust and adapt. The perspective is wonderful.

I remember Grandma Duncan telling me about the introduction of cold cereal. When it debuted it was touted as a health food and it was very expensive. As Sarah was one of ten, her parents could not afford to feed them all cold cereal. But she had a brother who was a well-known boy soprano in Glasgow, the child star of the family, so he got to have cold cereal while the rest of them had eggs. Sarah was sent off in the morning with a hot, hard-boiled egg in her pocket to keep her hands warm, and later she would eat it at school.

Reflection gives us perspective to separate then from now. Take what you learned from your upbringing and sort out what is helpful to you based on your current knowledge and circumstances. Discard any wrong beliefs you picked up about money, or the lack of it, along the way. Money is neutral. It isn't good or bad. It's not what money is, it's how you use it.

"Yes, wealth is a tool that gives you choices – but it can't compensate for a life not fully lived. The whole point of being alive is to evolve into the complete person you were intended to be."

Oprah Winfrey, *The Oprah Magazine September 2002*

And let's consider the example we set for children today. Wouldn't it be wonderful if children knew about the importance of money management at the same time they were learning about the importance of eating fresh vegetables at the dinner table? Even if you don't have young children, if you are an aunt or an uncle, or now you have grandchildren, you still set an example which can be very influential.

Often aunts, uncles and grandparents hold a special place in a child's heart simply because they are not Mom or Dad. My sister once jokingly said that if I ever had children, her children might become less special to me. There's an element of truth to that. For me, the best role in the world is being "Auntie Heather." I don't have children of my own and I don't interact with kids on a daily basis, so when I'm with my nieces or my nephew I become re-acquainted with their worldview. Their individual personalities and interests, their developing sense of who they are and what they love fascinates me. I'm completely captivated.

Children need "witnesses." They need adults in their lives other than Mom & Dad whom they can trust, and who know them; someone they can turn to when they need validation, a second opinion, a knowledgeable, honest and sympathetic ear. We witnesses carry a lot of weight. The other consideration is that the job of being Mom & Dad is already all-encompassing. Perhaps we can ease a bit of the burden of a parent's role by talking to the kids in our lives about the importance of working hard, saving and investing money wisely.

"It is like love; the more you give away, the more you get back. Your capacity for wisdom increases each time you share it with another. Those who are celebrated for their wisdom are those who have shared it freely to help others grow."

Chérie Carter-Scott, *If Life is a Game, These are the Rules*

Chapter 4

Anne B.

Anne is 53. She and her husband Jim are separated but currently share an apartment. They have a daughter, Alison.

Anne, tell me about going back to school?

I was 48 when I went back to school. Alison was leaving to go to university and Jim and I had separated a couple of years before. I had wanted to keep as much consistency in Alison's life as possible. We had moved many times and at one point we lost our home, but she always went to the same school. I felt free after Alison finished high school. I felt that I could do what I wanted to do now.

What brought you to that point?

When I was younger I always thought my mom should have done something else. She was very smart and a good person, but I always felt that she wasn't in the right place. She was 53 when my dad died and he was only 44. She had no skills, she worked but she didn't have a profession. She had taught in a one-room school but she never went to teachers college, and she said to me "always do something, have something to fall back on."

When I was a child, women didn't wear slacks. I can still remember sitting at the table watching mom at the kitchen sink. She had a nice little dress on because women only wore dresses then. She always looked neat and tidy and I can still remember thinking when I was sitting there as a child "Yup, that's what I'm going to do. When I grow up I'm going to get married and I'm going to wear nice little house dresses, and I'm going to have everything nice when my husband comes home." I clearly remember that and every time I think about it now I just about throw-up.

When I was 19 I worked for a summer at a factory because it was good money, which mom and I needed. I hated every second of every day. My boss asked me to come to the cafeteria and talk to him after I'd been there about a month. He said "you know, you shouldn't be working here. You just don't fit in a factory." I realized what he was saying. "I really do want to go back to school" and he said "you should go back to school, you're wasting your life here." That was pretty bold of him. This was a man talking to a teenage girl. He didn't have anything to gain by speaking to me, but maybe he had seen too many women settle for factory jobs. I think what he said was one of the nicest things anyone has ever done for me.

I was born and raised Catholic and back then you felt you had four or five choices: you finished high school, got married and had kids; you became a secretary; a teacher; a nurse or a nun. And university was for a few of the rich kids. After being out of school for three years, I took a one year course in what used to be called Medical Records and I worked really hard. Medical Records involved health and the hospital, it was administrative and technical. I remember saying to mom "I'm never going to want to do anything else, this is wonderful."

At 48 you moved to another city, went back to college, took a loan, and got on the Dean's list. It took a lot of gumption to do that. But there's a gap here.

Well, there's a big gap.   After I completed the Medical Records course in my twenties, I went to work at a large mental health facility away from home.   That's where I met Jim and we got married. We moved around a lot and Jim went back to school.   When I couldn't get work in Medical Records I went into real estate, but that's when interest rates went up to 27%. I loved it but I didn't make any money. I also worked at weight loss clinics which I loved too. But I worked at pieces of things. When I look back now I get so angry at myself and think: I could have finished a degree in all those years.

Now, life is better. I can't believe I'm back in a profession that I graduated from when I was 22 or 23, and I'm making the money I'm making. It's nice to have choices. I really gave it my all when I went back to school at 48.

You said to me, that your late forties was a time to channel your energies and your plans for how you were going to support yourself. At this point you were separated and you knew you didn't have any financial backing. Now you're working but you have quite a large loan to pay. You live in a bachelor apartment, you put money in your RRSP and you maintain a great attitude.

Before, I felt that I was living but I was spending every cent to survive. I felt if I made twice as much money I could still live on as little as before. I don't deny myself the way I used to because it is really foolish not to have some fun. But it doesn't have to cost a lot of money to have fun either. It's a bit discouraging if you start thinking about RRSPs at my age. They always say "well, if you do this, then ..." but don't even show me those graphs because I can't do that. It's past. Show me what I can do now. And I know I'm the type of person who will never not work. I'm going to do something.

Lot's of times I think it would be nice to work three days a week and maybe I'll do that after I'm 65.

Materially, you don't have a lot. I'm sure you acquired more possessions than I've seen in your apartment. Was there a shift in your thinking?

Oh yes. I love beautiful things and if I had the money I could go out and buy, but I don't feel the need to have them and I think that makes the difference. I love them, I go into peoples' homes and I really appreciate them, but I won't mortgage myself. I sold a lot of my possessions. Jim and I lost our house when mortgage rates were high and housing prices were low. We actually gave back the house and walked away from it, and I thought "this is never going to happen to me again. I'm never going to lose that kind of money again. I'm never going to be put in the position where I am trapped by someone or something. Never. Never."

This has happened many times throughout my life. This is what I'd really like to tell people: never go against what you truly feel. I can give you an example. When I was in real estate I would find a house and I would say to Jim, "we should buy it." We had a house but we could sell it and buy this other house and fix it up, then sell it and we'd make some money. Even at that time if you made $3,000 or $4,000 it was a lot of money. So 'grim reaper' Jim (to give him his due he's very practical and down-to-earth) would say "well, I don't know, you know it needs new wiring and new plumbing and …" He'd list all the negative things about it, and I would think "you know, he's probably right. I really shouldn't think about buying that house." A few years later, people had done exactly what I suggested to all the houses I'd picked-out, and they made a fortune.

I have a more aggressive personality than Jim's. People always told me I was too impulsive, so I really stomped on myself for a long time. When I see people who have a passion for things today I say "go for it." My God, do it even if you don't do it for very long. Do it. What's six months out of your life? Or a year?

And it's silly things. I wanted to buy an MG. I always wanted an MG sports car. I guess because my brother was a "car nut" and I thought he was the greatest thing since sliced bread, I got interested in cars. Everybody would say "well, you know I don't think you should buy an MG, because I had a friend who had to drop the transmission, and its really expensive, and you can't drive it in the winter and …blah, blah, blah." With all the negative statements I bought one anyway. It was the best thing I ever did in my life. I had so much fun with that car. I had it for two or three years and I never regret buying it.

So that was an instance where the negatives came out, but you chose to go with your gut?

Right! Because it was something I really wanted. And even if I had only owned it for a year it's not a big deal. I had a ball with that car. I loved it. My goal is to buy another.

I see you as a contradiction. You want another MG yet you can live so frugally.

It's true. (As long as I have books. I don't know what I would do if I didn't have access to a library.) I keep thinking OK, now I'm making money again as a Health Records Administrator because it really took me five years to update my skills and get where I am today (and I'm still updating them). So I can pay off my loan shortly and I will have no debt. And there is a need for what I do, especially in Ontario and across Canada. If I wanted to I could probably write to any town or city and I could have a job. That's pretty nice, especially after all the years I had jobs but no career.

Again, I would die if I couldn't work, if I couldn't do anything, although there are lots of times I think I would rather stay in bed thank you very much. In fact I even taught behaviour modification courses for a weight loss clinic, so you would think I could modify my own behaviour! I know all the tricks but you have to put them into practice. I have this aspect of my personality which says "I have to know." When I was very young I used to think of all the things I was never going to know, all the people I wouldn't meet and all the books I'd never read.

And look at Alison, she's finished one degree and she's thinking about another.

She doesn't work as hard as I do. It's true. I said to her, "if I had come to university and started at the same time and in the same kinesiology program as you did, I probably would have beaten your ass." She says "Yeah Mom, you're right." She has her degree but she could have had better marks. This kid was an honour's student in grade school, then in grade 7 she started sloughing off and it never got much better all through high school. The teachers and I would meet and talk with her. But you know, our children live by example; it's not that Jim and I were lazy but we were all over the place. Once she said to me as a teenager "well, I always saw you and Dad sort of getting by." I think what she was trying to say was she saw us going from one thing to another without really accomplishing anything, without getting ahead, but always "getting by." As parents, we really set the example. I don't think you have to have a fantastic job, but if I had been truly happy in what I was doing and if

30

I'd felt proud of myself that would have radiated out to the people around me.

My mom lived with us for three years before we lost the house. It was a really bad time and Jim's mom had had a stroke. Jim's mom could still live at home but she needed assistance and Jim went to live with her. That's sort of how we separated.

Now Jim and I share an apartment. Part of the reason I suggested he come to Ottawa is because I was having trouble with my periods and I had had a lot of tests. To make a long story short, I was told that I could have uterine cancer. So I dropped by a travel agency to find out how much it would cost to spend 3 or 4 weeks in Greece and Egypt which I wanted to do before I died. (I couldn't afford to go.) Jim's a really good guy and I knew he would look after me. So I thought if I'm dying and Jim came here, he and Alison would be in the same city. The thought of dying didn't bother me, I was very practical about it, but I knew I didn't want to be in pain and I'd have to set this straight with the doctors. I didn't want to live to be 99 anyway. Some of my feelings stemmed from thinking about my mom. She spent the last five years of her life in a nursing home with Alzheimer's and she didn't know who we were. I thought at least I won't have to spend the rest of my life like mom.

That was last year. I've since found out that I don't have cancer but in the meantime I had invited Jim to come and live with me. It's pretty funny but I don't even bother trying to explain because nobody in the world understands how he and I can live together in a bachelor apartment. For me he's safe and we like doing the same things. We both get up early. We both have a good relationship with Alison. He still annoys me to hell sometimes, but I think this arrangement helps me smooth over some of the guilt I feel about decisions we made in the past.

Again, if I gave anybody any advice I would say to never go against your feelings. It's a gut thing; it's intuitive, it's instinctive. I took a course called Streetproofing Your Child, and the facilitators said to pay attention to your "uh-oh feeling." If you think about it, it happens everyday to you in some way or another. It's more than just your conscience. And when you get that "uh-oh feeling" you don't do it. On the reverse side there's another feeling, and I don't know what you call it, but you just know it's the right thing to do. And if you go against this you're sunk. Women particularly have this intuitive talent and they have to learn to listen for it. If you start being aware you'll see you have it. The problem is that we women live our lives through everybody else. We've lived vicariously. For example, "behind every successful man is a woman" - it's true!

I would offer that piece of advice, and surround yourself with books, don't ever stop learning. And, choose your friends. Have someone who is at least at your intellectual level or greater, because you're going to strive. If you hang around with people who are smarter than you and have more knowledge of the world, you'll learn so much from them. All my friends are unique. If you got them in a room together you'd probably think they don't have anything in common.

You and Alison are friends too, aside from being mother and daughter. Financially, what do you want to tell her?

First of all, you have to save some of what you make. But if you have a real passion for something and you're happy doing it and you can support yourself, that's what counts.

32

What brought this home was Oprah (and you know she can get a bit spiritual sometimes). She was doing a story about this woman lawyer who'd be in her 40's, I guess. And from the time this lawyer graduated, for over 20 years, she's worked to fight for people to have decent places to live. This was somewhere in California where they have rats in tenement housing. She has spent every minute of her working life and more doing this. She makes just enough money to live on, she doesn't make big money. There's a little bit more to it, but she said "… happiness is not about money. Yes, you do have to support yourself, but if making money is all that counts that's not happiness." She could have a big mansion, she could have all kinds of stuff, but she's happy, happy.

I'm not trying to sound like a holier-than-thou person. As I said I'd love to have beautiful things but I don't need them. I think a lot of people need stuff, but I've been able to separate between need and want and I'm glad I can. I feel sorry for people who can't. I would figure I'm really destitute if I have no books and no friends. If I had all the money in world but I didn't have those things, it wouldn't count.

I would look at what's needed in the world, in today's society, and there's probably something that you could pick that you would like to work at, if you haven't found your passion yet. You choose that, you train for it, and work hard at doing it. You have to do your best. And you never stop learning.

It's good and it's nice to be financially secure but you could drop dead tomorrow. Old age and sickness and disability are good levelers, and death is the greatest leveler. I know having more money when you're older makes life a lot easier, but I think you have to balance it. If you have to work 60 hours a week to survive that's not good. I don't believe anybody should work that amount of time. I'm sorry, there's not enough time in your life. You might have to work those hours to get over a crisis, that's different. But I think people need time to cultivate friends, to cultivate more togetherness, to experience a sense of community.

I think I'm drawn to places like Mexico because people are community-minded. They haven't got anything but they get together, they have a fiesta and everybody goes. It was similar when I was young and we'd go to my relatives in Quebec for a shower. If you had a shower everybody went. The whole town would go, there might only be a couple of hundred people in the town but they'd all go. I miss that. Kids like my daughter have never experienced it.

Financially, I'd tell women to keep working. It's really hard for young women who get married and want to have a family. I never had to leave Alison at a babysitter's and I never regret being at home with her, but its such a chunk out of your life. Probably what I would recommend is doing something that you can do on your own time, or part-time so that you can still keep your career going. There's got to be something including taking courses, or if you have to, dragging your kid along. I think a young woman has to work really hard to get proper care for her children so that she can become a person, so she doesn't have to ride on the coattail of her husband or her kids.

I often look back and think "I wish I'd had a mentor." In a way, my mom was my mentor because she was a strong person. She worked really hard within the boundaries of her time. She didn't have the choices we have now. And it's so nice to have choices, to never back yourself into a corner. You always have a choice. I want to live the way I want to live and I want to be with the people I want to be with. I refuse to be with horrible people, because there are too many nice people, there are too many nice, interesting, wonderful people in the world.

Anne, any last comments?

Recognize your own patterns. You have to have a sense of humour and develop it. Know the difference between negativity and realism. Know yourself. Know what you can and cannot put up with. (I know I need a decent night's sleep.) Young women are not empowering themselves, they're relying too much on others to see them through. As you're living your life, think about how you want to look back on it. Will you feel satisfied with what you are doing? I know I wasted a lot of time. In the past I drifted. For the first time in all my life, I feel really powerful. I feel in charge of my life.

Chapter Five

Balance & Perspective

Ten years ago my childhood friend Roberta included me in a group of women who had been a part of her life, and she asked us each to be "honourary godmothers" to her first born daughter. As honourary godmothers it was our privilege to pass on to Ninka one piece of advice. I didn't have to think about mine. If I could make one wish for Ninka in her life ahead, it was that she would be able to find balance. That was my "godmother-wish" which I wrote to her. Each year, it seems an even more important quality to have and harder and harder to come by. To me, balance means being able to co-ordinate all the important aspects of one's self and one's life. It means having peace of mind, knowing what is of value to you; being able to fine-tune your daily life so that it encompasses a little bit of everything which is meaningful and excludes that which distracts or depletes. It is the process of being present and adaptable to today's circumstances without losing sight of future dreams and without losing touch with one's history and unique story. It definitely requires juggling, almost hour by hour, on a daily basis. It means saying yes, but more importantly, it means saying no without being overly apologetic, without regrets.

Sometimes I think we especially have to say "no" to information; "no" to being constantly bombarded with words and images which seek our attention. We give away our focus and our energy so easily. Have you ever thought *"I wonder what it would be like to go through a day without exposure to any advertising of any kind?"* I doubt there has been one single day in my life when I was not exposed to ads, logos, trademarks, brand names or signs; when I didn't overhear jingles, commercials, announcements ... attention K-Mart shoppers. We are all somebody's target market. We are each the pawn in somone's battle for market share.

As I was writing this section of the book, a client phoned because she'd heard on last night's news that mutual funds were going down in value. I told her that what she heard was an analysis of the previous month's statistics on all funds. I use the word "analysis" lightly because the only thing the commentator managed to do was strike fear into my client. I reassured her that yes, the previous month's markets had been down quite a bit which naturally affected the performance of mutual funds in general, however her own portfolio was up since I had seen her two weeks before. She felt much better. She said "Heather, why do they do this?" My reply was, "They want you to stay tuned to what they are saying so you will see the commercials which follow and hopefully buy the products. Then, because of course you want to be informed, you'll either keep watching or you will tune in again tomorrow to know the very latest." In other words, they need you to be hooked on information. In the most diplomatic way I could, I suggested that she re-direct her energy to the beautiful summer we were having and spending more time outside with her grandchildren.

For each of us, I offer this quote from one of my favourite books, *Simple Abundance: A Daybook of Comfort*

38

and Joy, written by Sarah Ban Breathnach and published by Warner Books.

> "But worries about money mock you. They steal the joy of living because they follow you around all day like a dark menacing shadow ... When you're worried about money you dread the days and you agonize at night. Without thinking, you throw away every precious 24 hours that comes your way ... When I surrendered my desire for financial security and sought financial serenity instead, I looked at my life with open eyes. I saw that I had much for which to be grateful. I felt humbled by my riches and regretted that I took for granted the abundance that already existed in my life ... Finally I came to an inner awareness that my personal net worth couldn't possibly be determined by the size of my checking account balance. Neither can yours."

Sometimes I don't want to be trying to live an "accomplished" life. I want to live a quiet life. I no longer want to strive to do the best I can at everything I do and feel that I'm never doing enough. Or, that it's never good enough. I have no obsessive quest for excellence, but then I don't really need "excellence" in my life; what I want is happiness and contentedness.

I don't get as much completed in the hour, the day, the week, etc. as I should, and I often feel that only a fraction of my activities were truly given the best effort I could muster. In my head I know I could have done a better job if I weren't so tired, if I'd been taking better care of my health, if I weren't preoccupied with everything else on my "to do" list. I could have been more focussed if I didn't owe family or friends a phone call, an email, a birthday wish, a word of reassurance or condolence, but most importantly if I didn't owe them what I really wanted to give them: my time and a listening ear. I could have been more efficient if the laundry basket wasn't overflowing, if there weren't groceries rotting in the fridge, if the bathroom wasn't calling out to be cleaned.

I'd like to do less. I'd like to have a contemplative, appreciative life. I want to sit by the window and look out at the rain or the snow. I want to sit, be grateful and imagine. Imagine being a pioneer. Imagine being without warmth, protection, or any food you could want at anytime. I want to look down at the comfy clothes I am wearing and imagine the garments I'd have on my body as a settler. Imagining not only how those garments would have felt: rough, damp, either too hot in the summer or too cold in the winter, stained and dirty, but also how they would have smelled? Can you imagine having to think about how to stay alive? How would you keep the others alive and the animals you depended on too? How would you keep hazards and perils at bay? You could never take a day off. To be alive another day meant you had to stay alive another day.

Then I think about who and where I am, and I'm so appreciative. How lucky I was to be born in the latter half of the 20th century, to be born in Canada. I've never been without a roof over my head. For sure I've been down to my last few dollars, especially as a university student, but not as a resident of a shelter or as person living on the street, begging and surviving. I've always had the ability to earn an income. I've never been starving or deathly ill. I haven't experienced tragedy in my life, yes definitely loss and heartbreak, disappointment, sadness and depression, but not tragedy. Love doesn't protect you from hurt. I have been loved my whole life. I've never lived through war, drought or famine. I have no experience with any of those things. I've never been persecuted. I've never been raped, imprisoned or enslaved. When I think of the whole history of

40

humanity, I am so thankful. I was born in a country of abundance, in a time of relative peace. I have had every opportunity. I want to live simply, with health and peace of mind, to spend hours thinking, wondering and being aware, and therefore to spend my time being grateful.

I've flown over the Andes at sunrise. I have attended the birth of a child and seen the look on his face as he entered the world. I've experienced the trust of babies and the unconditional love of children. I've watched the vibrant colours of a sunset shift over Georgian Bay. I've seen the most luminous, beautiful pearl: a full moon in a navy-blue sky outside my own back door. I've known and admired people who, in their old age, shared their thoughts and feelings with me as their life wound down. I have observed the grace of animals in their natural habitat, which made me feel like the alien that I was. I've had memorable meals. I've laughed so hard with friends we wanted to cry. I've completed a marathon without properly training for it (one of my less brilliant ideas). I have been welcomed into peoples' homes, at their tables, into their hearts. And every single day, the beauty of the planet blows me away. It only takes a cloud in the sky, a maple leaf in the wind, the sound of the mourning dove, the red-winged black bird, or a loon on a lake. I am blessed.

I want to go placidly. I don't want to win awards for having done or accomplished so much. Not that I'm in the running for anything! I want to do less not more. A subtle legacy is a good legacy; that friends and family and perhaps a few others knew a peaceful soul lived here. Why do we think that without fame, publicity, medals, awards, articles, appointments, accolades, plaques, Oscars or Emmys we aren't accomplished at anything? That without recognition, we somehow haven't measured up?

41

Chapter Six

Jackie M.

Jackie was widowed at 60. Her husband Frank had two daughters from his first marriage, and he and Jackie had three daughters together.

I hope women will pick up this book and realize they are not alone or recognize that someone has been in a similar situation; they may think if she can get through that, I can get through this.

If I was talking to anyone, I would tell them it is a great thing to have a financial planner to take charge of the investments.

I was desperate when my husband died. He had committed suicide and it was like an explosion in the family. The result was I was left alone in a big house, in the country, in the winter and I can't drive. I was alone with Frank's dog – and the dog was upset and unruly. It was a kind of nightmare.

Frank's daughter came from Toronto and she took over more or less. All I could do was cry. I could hardly remember my name. I had no bank account of my own. I had saved money for Christmas so I had about $400. The payments for the house were taken out of Frank's bank account and I had no idea where anything was. He had paid all the bills. Maybe it was his generation – it meant a lot to Frank that he had control of financial things, where we lived, that sort of thing.

Perhaps he thought he was looking after you. But it wasn't helpful, because when he died you had to learn very quickly.

And it wasn't the best of times. The stress – it's like your brain is not functioning. I have been told by women who have lost their husbands "don't take one step in any direction for at least two years. Don't make decisions."

I've heard that before and I think it's true. But that's only useful for someone whose situation is fine and you can maintain the status quo for two years. That wasn't your case, you had to make decisions. You didn't have a choice.

And I was worried. For example, Frank had a car and a pick-up truck, and today I have no idea where the truck went. Frank had many tools, and a very kind friend of Frank's came to the basement and he sold as much as he could of Frank's equipment so I could have some cash. A nice gentleman found a family for Frank's dog.

Little by little I started coming out of the fog. I knew I was by myself, that I was alone and had to rely on myself. We heated the house by wood so I had to bring the wood in, and clean the driveway, and I did it. I went to see a lawyer and he steered me as best he could to do the right thing. He made an application so I could get some pension money. Frank owed money to his accountant and the lawyer settled that. The lawyer was extremely kind and I was lucky. At the time I didn't appreciate his kindness, but I do now.

Did Frank have a will?

Yes, Frank had a will. He had insurance but since he had committed suicide that was cancelled. There was a note. There was no insurance, but there was a certain amount of money, I don't remember where it came from, to cover the funeral expenses.

After the funeral, I thought I had to find someone to talk to. I didn't have any close friends. I was friendly to the neighbours and they had been very helpful with the funeral, but I didn't feel I could bother them now. At that point I was really desperate, at the end of my rope. I looked in the phone book and I found a number for an organization with the name "Family Focus" so I called. A woman by the name of Joanie answered. I was crying and crying and she said just tell me where you live. Even though there was a snowstorm she came to my house as soon as she could. She was a social worker. She calmed me down and I felt that I had some contact with somebody. Joanie organized all kinds of meetings for Family Focus and she would come and pick me up and take me there. There was a gang of women and 3 or 4 fellows who attended these meetings, and for some reason being with people who also had things to deal with made me feel better. They weren't sad; it was cheerful. It was something I obviously needed. I had a certain will to survive this, to survive what I had been through.

And then you found you had to sell your home?

[Slowly Jackie nods.] It sold very easily. I'm just getting over the loss of my garden. I had put all my energy into it. I still think about it. I had a vegetable garden and lots of raspberries. I had about an acre so I had lots of room to experiment. I grew delphiniums and asparagus which I had started from seed.

I had a mortgage on the house. One thing I remember now is that I had $12,000 owing on the house. After Frank's death and items had been sold I had the money to pay-off

45

the mortgage. The woman at the bank didn't want me to pay it off. I guess it was in the bank's best interest for me to keep the mortgage. It didn't take much, but she was able to intimidate me. I was very easily intimidated. I couldn't argue with her. The $12,000 that wasn't used against the mortgage was more or less frittered away in nonsense. Before I decided to sell the house, someone said I needed a new roof. Maybe I did, maybe I didn't. "And you need this and you need that." That money was wasted really. We'd been in the house about 15 years so it was fairly new.

Did you know it was time to sell because of the upkeep or was it too hard because of the memories?

No, it was because I couldn't drive and I didn't want to drive. I desperately wanted to keep my house. I took in a border. I thought, "Oh, the neighbours are going to talk!" I thought I was making a deal with him, and in exchange for a small amount of room and board he would drive me when I needed to go somewhere. I was so relieved when the boarder moved in. I cannot tell you the difference between being in that house by myself and having someone there, anyone there. And that first summer he did a lot of gardening. But it was a bad situation. He had no intention of paying room and board. He took advantage of my being so easy to maneuver. It was all stupidity and I'm ashamed of myself now.

I was lucid enough that I knew what was going on. But I wanted him to be there so I could stay in my house. I was used to depending on Frank and now I was depending on this person. He treated me horribly. For some reason I know that in spite of everything, I think he was there for a reason and he did help me in many ways. I had to learn a lesson. And of course now I'm not so easily naïve. Today, I can still consider him a friend. He's very nice now, he wouldn't dream of acting the way he did then.

That's very strong of you.

I'm trying to excuse myself. Emotionally I wasn't very well. I realize that now. Any man, he could have had three heads … In my mind I was thinking if he had three heads and he could drive, I could keep my house. It did come to a point where I realized that it wasn't going to be possible. I sold the house and I put the money in my account. And then I met you, and things started going much better.

Good things can come out of bad circumstances.

Always. You have to trust people.

It's something we have to re-learn. People can let us down and we have to try again. The woman in the bank didn't make you feel tall, she made you feel small. But you went out on a limb to meet with me, a financial planner.

If you were to give this book to a young woman, let's say a granddaughter one day, what would you want her to know?

Even if you think it is distasteful, you have to think of your financial situation and not depend on anyone. Always remember in the back of your mind that you are an individual and you should be independent. If you want to be with someone there is nothing wrong with that, it's wonderful. But anything can happen. My comfortable life changed in five seconds. You may emotionally depend on someone but money and emotions are two different things. Money and emotion don't have much to do with each other. Money is like a tool, it's like a shovel or a hammer. You go with the best tool.

47

You've come a long way Jackie.

I had lots of lessons to learn in this life. We do have lessons to learn.

What are you learning these days?

To take things more easily, and to be more accepting of my shortcomings. To be more kind to myself. If I'm messy or lazy in my apartment, it's OK. I forgive other people, why shouldn't I forgive myself? I like to go out to garage sales on the weekends. I'm a maniac for garage sales. Garage sales and the Sally Ann [The Salvation Army], those are my two places where I like shopping. I like painting, and artistic things. And books – I like to read.

Every time I come to see you, you look a little bit younger. But how do you know that you're feeling stronger, that you're coping well?

Because I'm kinder. In my heart, I feel kind towards people. If you're depressed you tend to be inside of yourself. You don't necessarily say anything, but you see the bad side of things. And now my heart is kinder. If you see someone who is grouchy and unhappy, or you see someone who is impatient, I think it is because they are not feeling good inside. If you feel good, you're going to be patient.

Considering that you didn't handle the finances before your husband died, there has been a big change. When we meet you have all your papers in files.

Yes, I'm surprised at that too. But I know if I don't do that trouble is going to be a hundred times worse. So you do what you have to do, at least the minimum.

We went through your taxes line by line this year and you were more attentive than many of my clients. You were asking questions and each year you know a little bit more.

It has a certain logic to it. And I think if I put my mind to it, I will understand it, that it's not that difficult. Anything can be understood if you want to take the time and effort to understand it. But to me, numbers, well taxes aren't sexy.

No, they're not sexy. I'm glad you brought that up.

I know that I'm doing the minimum at least: not to incur debt, to pay my bills on time, and to know what is in the bank. There is something I want a lot, it's not a car, it's a kind of sewing machine for some ridiculous price like $3,000. OK, maybe I don't want it that badly. You put a little disk in it and it does all kinds of things. They show it on TV and they make the commercials so you'll want the darn thing! But I can understand that it's just not necessary for me.

You get more satisfaction from living within your means than from making large purchases.

It's peace of mind. If you don't pay your phone bill they're going to turn the phone off.

I know you're still scarred from your husband's death and the way he died.

If its someone you love very much, you feel that you let him down. I knew there was something very, very bad going on. It was almost as if he was retreating into himself even more. I couldn't talk to him. He didn't want me to get close to him at all. So you have this feeling … it was like ice, you could almost feel cold coming out of him. I tried to ask him. He was a man, I guess, who thought he had to be strong. He

49

had to be a man who looked after everything. I always thought he did okay.

After the funeral, the next day or so, somebody came to the door. It was a young man who had a photography store and Frank used go there to have pictures made, so I guess they were friends. I didn't know this man but he came to my house and he wanted to talk to me. He said, "I have to tell you something." He said "I was meditating and I heard Frank's voice in my head telling me 'go tell my wife I'm okay'." I thought that young man had a lot of courage to risk passing for an idiot who hears voices. It was so touching, but there are little kindnesses like that that people do. It did make me feel better.

It's hard to lose your husband too young. Most of us have this idea of having some really nice, happy retirement years together because we spend so long working towards it. When it's suicide there must be other emotions and feelings you have to adjust to as well.

You take it by stages. You deal with one thing. It's a series of losses. Losing a husband, losing family, losing the garden. And I had to stop looking for Frank, he's gone. That's the message I got in my dreams, it's like your subconscious is working to help you. In my dream I was looking for him, we were in a big building and we had gotten separated and I was looking everywhere. I realized I was not going to find him. So gradually you get settled into the fact that he is gone.

You are saying that over time you adjust to different "facts" of the whole picture, you don't adjust to the whole picture all at once.

No. I remember the garden wasn't as important to Frank as it was to me. My home could be a prison, but I made my garden a paradise. I remember when I said "OK, now this is gone." I don't think I could have done it all in one fell swoop. It's been four years since Frank died and I had stayed in the house for over a year after his death.

Then you moved to a small apartment in a small town and now you've moved to an apartment in a bigger town.

There are more possibilities here. Who knows, I might become quite bold and take a bus somewhere. My independence is something I have to lift, being able to do more things, and meet people. There are some very nice people in this building, and lots of widows. No matter how a husband dies, its hard when you lose your husband. Whether he has been sick for years or dies suddenly, it's a terrible blow. You can't understand until you know what it's like, because you seem to grow together, its almost like one person. We were together for 40 years. I started going out with him when I was 19. All my woman-years were with him, and he was a nice man. Life sometimes gnaws at you. His self-esteem had been terribly, terribly damaged for a long time, because of work.

A lot of our self-esteem comes from work. When our work situation changes it can really affect us because we don't separate who we are as people from who we are in the roles we have.

He always did the best he could. He lost his job twice. It's a very tricky world. Things go up and down all the time. I think emotion is mixed up with money.

You made an excellent point earlier about learning to separate money and emotion. Learn to see money as a tool "like a shovel or a hammer" as you put it.

It's nothing more than that. If its more than that, that's where you make mistakes. For me it's such a relief to have given myself that perspective. Money is nothing more than what it is, it's not love. Your security is inside yourself. Especially in this country, you'll never go begging for food. So you deal with money in a responsible way. I think some people are playing games with money. You shouldn't do that.

The other fear is the gambling culture we're developing with the casinos and the lottery tickets.

And people kill themselves. It happened recently in the parking lot of a casino. I heard that since they opened a casino in Quebec, thirty men have committed suicide because of gambling. I guess they gambled to the point where their money was all gone or they took other people's money. Suicide is not that common but it's not that rare either. Some people don't expect anything good to happen because they don't think anything good ever did. It's sad. I don't judge. We can't know what's inside another person. Maybe Frank did the best he could do, but I think he would be sorry he committed suicide. Personally, I think he would regret having done that.

I believe that most of the time, we really do try to make the best decisions we can, with what we know.

Yes, that's true. Even if it turns out not to have been a good decision. When you are faced with something you react. And sometimes it's not the best, but you did the best you could.

I have a feeling too that there's a lot of loneliness for women my age. I can cope with my loneliness, it's not so much loneliness as being alone. I had not thought about myself as an individual for years. Things were just going the way they always had, it was like a routine, and I didn't have to think about myself. So this is a new hobby, being reflective. Dwelling, yes why not? It could be interesting.

I think of my grandmothers, they were both widowed for over 30 years. Grandma Duncan used to do volunteer work at a cancer clinic. The extent of her job was pouring tea for people. It meant so much to her to put on her daffodil-yellow volunteer uniform. She did it into her eighties and she got a lot of satisfaction from helping others.

And there are always people asking for volunteers. That's something I would be interested in. Maybe reading to children, because they love that. Kids are so full of life and pep, and they're curious.

Chapter Seven

Financial Planning = Stress Relief

"Wise men and women in every culture throughout history have found that the secret to happiness is not in getting more but in wanting less."

Elaine St. James, *Simplify Your Life*

How do you know when you are doing good financial planning? You will know because you'll feel like a million bucks even if you're not worth a million bucks, yet. You will feel light, energetic, productive, happy and hopeful; it should feel as though you have lost 10 lbs. In a sense you have — ten pounds of stress. It should feel like a Saturday morning in the sunshine, in your favourite bath robe with a hot cup of tea or coffee, the Saturday paper, a magazine or a good book. It should feel that relaxed. No sense of panic, desperation or fear of the unknown, but rather a sense of calm, understanding and preparedness.

Is there such a thing as peace of mind when it comes to one's finances? Peace of mind comes from knowing you have addressed the main areas of financial planning as best you can for yourself and within your circumstances. It has to do with being aware of and looking at those aspects which are appropriate for you. If you try to keep up with the Joneses, you will drive yourself crazy because they're trying to keep up with the Smiths, who are trying to keep up with

Lamberts who are tying to keep up with the Chens who are trying to keep up with the Griffins, etc. You get the picture. You want to review the areas of financial planning which affect you every six months to a year, sort of like an annual check-up or dental appointment, and make changes as needed. In the meantime, you live within your means and stick to your plans as best you can, in the same way that between doctor and dental appointments we try to live a healthy life, get plenty of exercise and rest, brush & floss regularly.

Financial planning is not designed to add to your daily stress but to reduce it. Actually I much prefer the term "financial wisdom." Your financial picture is a snapshot in time. It's the same with your health. Life is not static.

Have you ever seen a friend and asked how they're doing and they said "fine." They look fine, but in the course of conversation you realize that wasn't the case. I hadn't seen Barry for a few months and when we got together I discovered he'd had an unexpected triple bypass. The operation took place shortly after our last meeting and now he was standing in front of me telling me he was fine and he was. In fact he joked he was actually in better shape than before – sort of "new and improved."

You and I don't want to wake-up every morning and wonder whether today is the day we are going to need triple bypass surgery. In the same way, our financial plan is not a house of cards. We've given thought and consideration to our plan. We've built in a reserve and flexibility. Our plan is not easily blown away. We can address issues if and when they come up.

Normal, healthy individuals who check themselves in the mirror every day for signs of cancer, who fear they may be developing ailments based on articles or TV shows, who are convinced that something will adversely affect them and they need to catch it early, are what health professionals call the "worried well." Many of us can take on the same attitude and behaviour when it comes to our finances. We need to stop that. We need to recognize that change in our circumstances, life and the world is a given. We need to trust ourselves and our ability to take responsibility for our financial well being with the help of other professionals, just as we look after our health.

> **"If one doesn't have a character like Abraham Lincoln or Joan of Arc, a diet simply disintegrates into eating exactly what one wants to eat, but with a bad conscience."**
>
> Maria Augusta Trapp, *The Story of the Trapp Family Singers*

Does the thought of financial planning cause you to panic? Do you get anxious when you contemplate your current circumstances or when you look down the road you are traveling? Do you become paralyzed at the thought of doing what you know you should do? When your thinking is not clear, does it feel like a broken record repeating itself over and over in your head?

When you are feeling overwhelmed, then don't underestimate the power of having a shower or taking a bath, of going for a walk or a run. At first the goal is to move your focus from the mental to the physical. To get out of your head and notice the physical sensation of being in water, or feeling your body moving through the air. You need to get distracted.

57

Having a shower or a bath can never be a neutral experience. A shower is cleansing, a bath is caressing. With a shower you get to imagine your worries being washed away. You actually see the soapy suds moving toward the drain and you picture your cares and troubles going with them. A warm bath in a quiet, dimly lit room is such a peaceful experience. Once you are in this place that physically feels good, comforting or refreshing, you can explore your thoughts anew. In fact, this time you can almost explore them from an out-of-body perspective.

The activity of walking is natural to us and yet there was a period in our lives when we struggled to do this. We have no memory of how many times we fell on our rump or flat on our face while trying to accomplish this feat. As adults we have seen toddlers ('toddler' is such an apt description) give it their all learning to stay upright and we know we did that too. Can a human being ever learn to walk without making a gargantuan effort? I wonder if in our subconscious we always think of that as our first, great achievement. Now as stressed adults we go for a walk to clear our heads. Maybe we want to go back to that initial feeling of accomplishment. What drove us instinctively as infants to learn to walk, even though it seemed like an impossible skill to master at the time? It must have been the desire for freedom and independence.

I think we're pretty smart now as adults to walk outside and feel nature on our face whenever we need to get a new perspective. The next step is going for a jog or a run. Not only do you experience the benefits of walking but you also get to feel your heart pumping, and you know oxygen-rich blood is coursing through your veins. The way a shower cleanses your outer body, a run cleanses your inner body. You can imagine that your running shoes are big erasers you've laced to the bottom of your feet; they cushion each step and erase your stress in the process. The secret is to first get your mind distracted and then allow the solutions to your concerns to bubble-up. Rather than trying to figure out the answer or the right action to take, let the answer come to you as you distract yourself doing something else. Some of my best ideas have come to me in the shower, while going for a run, or believe it or not, when doing the dishes by hand – the dishwasher doesn't have the same effect!

How does all of this relate to financial planning? Because how often have your thoughts, concerns and anxieties been intertwined with your financial situation? Or the financial situation of your children, your parents, your spouse or even your siblings? Exactly. For me the secret of having a bath or a shower, going for a walk or a run, is to come away with a clear idea of the next three steps I'm going to take, or projects I'm going to tackle. Before you pull the plug in the bathtub ask yourself, "What 3 things am I going to do next?" And don't get out until you've answered that question. It doesn't matter whether they're from your short-term to-do list or one of your long-term goals. Your actions will automatically serve you.

It's so hard to do everything right. There are so many things we could be doing, should be doing. Clients often say, "I know I should have met with you sooner, or handled this differently or dealt with such and such an issue a long time ago." But think of how much you juggle in a day. How many choices, decisions and responsibilities do you face? If you are not independently wealthy and living a life of leisure, then reflect on all you do and give yourself credit. I've read that being a perfectionist doesn't make you perfect, it makes you miserable. We all should have done more and better financial planning a lot sooner, myself included. It takes time to become financially wise.

No matter where your own area of experience, expertise or wisdom lies, you didn't get there overnight. Financial wisdom encompasses the passage of time – we continually get to learn from our mistakes and successes, it never stops. But with maturity and experience comes the wisdom to make fewer mistakes for your self and to enjoy more successes. If you know you are going to make some mistakes along the way, you can spend less time worrying about when the mistakes will occur. It doesn't matter, you just know they will. But you can spend more time structuring your plan to build upon your past successes and to insure that when a mistake does occur it isn't life altering. You will want to focus on a balanced and diversified financial plan as opposed to the perfect financial plan.

It is important to live within your means, to cover your bases, and to do the best planning you can. After that, you say a prayer, or make a wish, and get on with your day. You already have many accomplishments under your belt and there is so much more you want to see and do. It makes sense too, that we benefit from each other's knowledge and experiences. Or as I once read somewhere: Learn from other people's mistakes, because you can't live long enough to make them all yourself.

I'm not suggesting that we compare ourselves to others. If we were meant to be comparable we all would have been made the same or similar, cut from the same cloth. We're not. But we can use others' stories to inspire us and to teach us. Sometimes we don't appreciate certain people until years later when we look back and realize how often they are still in our minds and we wonder "Why do I still think about that person?" Then we can acknowledge the impact of that individual. It could have been somebody we were close to, or someone we've never met, but read about.

Maybe the experiences of a former colleague stays with you, or the philosophy of a teacher. I remember a math teacher – I think it was in junior high school – who first exposed me to the idea that time is like money, in that time is valuable and you choose how you want to spend it. He treasured time. When you are a teenager, the idea of treasuring something you've never even given any thought to, can be a pretty radical concept.

When I worked in consulting, I had a colleague who'd come from Germany and wanted to work in Toronto for two years. As a single person, she discovered that the rest of us single people worked too long and then had no life or involvement in our community at the end of the day. She found herself falling into our pattern of "flexible work hours" which just meant that as a salaried-employee you could work as many hours of overtime as you liked. If you wanted to maintain your position in the company and receive an annual increase, let alone succeed and be promoted, you had to put in the hours. Or as she explained, if she left at 5 o'clock she had to have two glasses of wine when she got home before she could get over the guilt of leaving on time. In less than two years she returned to Germany. I can't remember the name of my teacher or my colleague, but they each taught me valuable lessons, which I sometimes have to re-learn the hard way. And when I do, I think of them and I'm glad they crossed my path.

One more point regarding health and wealth and the idea that financial planning equates to stress relief: we can't put off financial planning for ourselves until everyone else is looked after. Financial planning is too important, it's the flip side of our health. We don't say "I won't look after my health right now. Once the kids are through school then I'll eat fresh fruit and make sure I get minerals and vitamins, sleep and some exercise." But we do that when it comes to our finances.

Many of us, men and women, are guilty of this line of reasoning. In essence, we think: I can't start saving the money I'll need to support myself in the last thirty years of my life (when my medical needs and care expenses could be very high) until after my kids are out the door and on their own, until everyone else is looked after. Then, when I only have ten to fifteen working years left I'll start trying to squirrel away everything I'll need for the remaining thirty years of my life. It's not that we're stupid or unreasonable, we're not. But we can be unrealistic and we get so distracted making sure everyone else is okay that we start thinking our long-term needs are secondary to the immediate and short-term needs of others. They're not.

Not only do we need to be putting money aside for our final years before we get there, but we also need to be aware of the fact that we could reach old age, with few other resources to assist us. I've seen the situation more than once, where all of the resources, including emotional energy and joint savings, are spent on the first spouse to become ill and/or incapacitated in retirement. If you are a woman with a spouse who is even a few years older than you, this could be a real concern. If the joint savings are depleted by the care of the first spouse, especially when you consider the cost of living in a nursing home for several years before death, where does that leave the second spouse who is now widowed? If her husband was lucky enough to have a company pension, the surviving spouse is at best receiving two-thirds of his pension, but her living expenses are almost the same. It will cost her the same in property taxes, maintenance and rent to remain in their home or apartment. Now she no longer has the cost of his care, but with their savings gone, who is going to provide for the cost of her infirmity in a few years time? Will she be able to rely on her children who may have their own financial worries? What if she doesn't have children or they live in another province or country? What if her children don't understand her situation or the family relationship has been strained beyond repair?

It doesn't seem fair, does it? That's why we want to be able to talk about these issues freely and be willing to look at our circumstances and address our concerns. If your gut is telling you that down the road you could be in trouble financially, then the thought of that future stress you will experience is causing you stress now. Let's deal with the stress by reviewing some options and taking action in the present, not waiting until the future. We can alter our actions as we go; progressively making the changes we need to make. I must admit, we all have the tendency to be ostrich-like. But if we encourage each other to pull our heads out of the sand and face reality today, we will be much happier, energetic and more productive ostriches tomorrow!

"You know, in five years, you can either be five years older or five years older with more passion, living more richly … the choice is yours, and it will be determined by what you do, not what you want."

David Bach, *Smart Couples Finish Rich (Canadian Edition)*

Chapter Eight

Fern W.

Fern is 58 years old. She is a doctor. She is divorced and she does not have children.

You are medical doctor by training but you don't have a family practice, tell me about your practice.

I think the theme of planning your life is sometimes based on education and I must admit education was certainly stressed in my family because my parents were first generation immigrants. My dad was raised for part of his life in Poland and came from a very poor station. He and my mother wanted to make a better life for their children and grandchildren. How I came to do what I do was actually evolutionary. I first became a chemist, then I got a graduate degree in physiology and bio-chemistry, and because I wanted to do clinical research I had to get an M.D. Once I got my M.D., I wanted to prove I could be a real doctor and not just a doctor through academia. So off I went to become a real doctor.

And the truth is that at this point I had to make some money. I owed a *lot* of money although I did have some scholarships. After nine years of university I was ready to go into the world, pay back some loans, start living a bit and having some fun. I was a family doctor in a part of Toronto called the Jane-Finch corridor which was a very tough neigbourhood. When I was in practice there, in the late seventies, it was burgeoning with very little social support so it was a highly troubled area with a high rate of crime.

I loved medicine but I found that I was doing as much social work as I was medicine. Eventually I became more interested in what made people the way they were than the diseases I was treating them for. I had a series of chance meetings including meeting a senior psychiatrist who worked with people who had survived massive events in their life, like the Holocaust. I had become interested in people's reactions, especially to the high trauma they were experiencing in the Jane-Finch corridor. I very much resisted going back to school because I'd had it, but somehow or other I got persuaded to work as a family doctor and go to school part-time to become a psychologist.

It was really difficult because I felt I still needed to make money but I also wanted to study so I was carrying a double load. But having done it, and made it, my practice is exclusively a psychotherapy practice. I have a subspecialty working with and helping people who have survived massive psychic trauma including those who've survived Eastern European concentration camps as well as other aspects of the Holocaust such as the experience of second generation trauma. There are some very unique problems that go with the second generation of families who themselves have no families. It doesn't mean to say that all concentration camp survivors have problems. They have what I would call "normal problems" – problems anyone would have who had experienced what they did.

From that work, many other patients have come to me who've survived similar massive trauma which I guess means the world hasn't learned very much. We still have areas of the world at war, practicing some form of genocide or some form of ethnic cleansing. So I now have people in my office from troubled places like Cambodia, Bosnia, Sarajevo, Kosivo and Rwanda. I also see combat and torture survivors from South America. In our society, unfortunately there is always sexual and physical abuse, mostly of women but I see a few men as well who have been very badly traumatized by their families, by some member of their family or perhaps by a neighbour.

This is the kind of work I do, which I love very much. In terms of money, I certainly would have made a lot more as a family doctor. It's much easier to see five cases of recovering tonsillitis in one half hour, and you get paid more for those five cases than you do for an hour of psychotherapy. Psychotherapy is hard slogging with a person who has a lot to come to terms with.

Do you see money as being a source of stress for the people in your practice?

It is for a number of them, yes. Some of them are people that have recently arrived and they have to scramble to make a living.

Lately, I've been ill and I've had women come to my house because I needed home care. A number of them are women of colour who've come from terrible spots in the world. One young woman is from Eritrea, another from Cambodia. I listen and I get a glimmer of what they've been through; they don't even realize they are heroines. Now they work at the lowest end of the pay scale in the home health-care field. They probably would be doing something else had they been allowed to stay in their country. They are bright, they are good at what they do, they are kind in how they do it, but they don't make much money at it.

I have had a few homemakers, either from the Islands or from troubled spots, who have absolutely amazed me. One young woman is going to school from 9 to 3 to get her nursing degree, working part-time as a homemaker (she works with a full heart when she comes to help me) and has one-year old twin boys. She does have a husband who is also working but it is a struggle for them. That kind of ambition is amazing to me. The kind of organization these women have to put into their lives is also heroic, yet they are just working to make ends meet.

So, yes money is really a problem. I've met other people who came from countries like Russia whose whole economic structure fell apart. There is a surgical nurse who is working full-time as well as part-time doing visiting nursing. She has a child and she's working to get her Masters degree. Money is definitely a problem. I'd say these women are in their thirties and probably at their prime but working immensely hard to get ahead. And they are not really saving - it's nice to advise people to save but they are doing all they can to get by and further their education.

Also, people who have been very badly abused, often women who have been sexually abused, or people who have survived a very humiliating trauma when they were young have very low self-esteem so they don't go into major professions which would give them a good sense of who they are. On the other hand, I have seen the opposite where the struggle was so severe the result was a very hardened commitment never to be at anybody's mercy again. I have seen people who have achieved a great deal but they have been driven by a hard-edged emotion which stems from the fear of ever being in a vulnerable position again.

By having money, that certainly leaves you less vulnerable in our society.

I have to apply that to myself. I am the child of immigrants who lived through the depression. Because of their experience they came to this country. I have had a much better opportunity than they ever had in terms of both the country in which I was born, but also the time in which I was born. I wasn't born in a depression, I was born in a post-war boom, so I was very fortunate even though I still had to borrow a lot of money to get through school. But the emphasis was exactly that: "Don't be vulnerable, get yourself an education. You call the shots in terms of your earnings and what you are going to do in life." Of course it doesn't completely work out that way. We never can call the shots all of the time.

My profession has allowed me to work in a way that I can be compensated but I am also compensated in terms of the meaningfulness of my work. For me, working as a family doctor wasn't as meaningful as being able to help people who have suffered in the way they have. So I chose to compromise income in order to do the work I do. And even though I'm not making the money that a lot of MD's are, when you look at other populations, I'm probably wealthier than 95 percent of the women in the world.

With respect to building and feeding a nest egg, the real concern is that women are living longer. You see this in your own family, as both your parents are still alive.

Absolutely. My message has always been to women that we don't look for the knight in shining armour. The reality is the knight in shining armour probably drives a Honda and needs help with the payments. I think every individual should know how to take care of himself or herself and not be beholden to anybody else, not be dependent on anybody else. If you want a relationship, have it for the relationship itself rather than for what kind of financial gain you can get from a partner. And usually it's women wanting more money from a more financially secure man. My advice is to look after yourself and start learning early. I think that I would be a lot more secure had I started looking at my finances in a more organized way at a younger age. But, thank God, I learned it when it wasn't totally too late.

It's interesting, I have a number of girlfriends my age and they are very practical - pragmatic I should say about how their lives are going to be. One of them in particular who has an exceptionally good marriage is also realistic about the fact that women outlive men. She is talking about all of us women friends preserving our health because she says she still wants us to be around for each other when our husbands are gone. She is sensible and I don't think it sounded at all macabre coming from her. But part of that means that we'll have to be financially independent to be able to enjoy some of the things we've worked for all our lives. I don't know how practical it is for someone who is 20, whether they could ever see being 40, let alone 70 or 80 or 90. But it's valuable advice.

For those of us who are in our forties now, 70 is looking more real, however we don't think of that as old age any more because we're closer to it!

But I don't even think its old age in terms of what we used to know as "old age." Our vision or idea of what a 70 year old looked like and behaved like a generation ago is not the same as now. There are women in their sixties starting new careers or settling into their crafts or art and developing those skills. Some of them are making money at it and some of them are merely enjoying the creative process, but they're not just dabbling. Nevertheless, I think those women are grateful they've got money with which to pursue their interests in their later years.

You've linked together health and finances. If we look after our health we're less likely to be dependent on health care services, which are increasingly more expensive. In other words, by maintaining our health, we're saving ourselves money aren't we?

I agree with you. We are. If we don't take care of our hearts and our bones, we're going to need more help instead of being able to do things on our own. It's automatically going to cost more. For example, we may not be able to do our own driving. Do you remember the film "Driving Miss Daisy"? Well, she was a wealthy widow and she could afford to have a driver, but we can't all have that.

From my own experience, as you know, I've had some serious health problems. Everything takes longer, and it costs more to get it done. To a certain extent, time is money. You just can't do things as efficiently. Regarding long-term health, taking care of our hearts and bones will save us so much in terms of physical pain and disability. It will allow us to move around and in a much better way. It will absolutely save us dollars in the end. My advice is to do everything you can to stay out of the health care system rather than in it. Even though some of the services we receive may still be subsidized, nevertheless, it is better to stay out. That means looking at a commitment towards yourself and your own health. If you are in your twenties and you have student debt, putting money aside at this point (as much as you would like to) isn't realistic for your circumstances. However, you can still be helping yourself financially down the road by looking after your health.

Do you have any thoughts to share on debt?

When I was in my late twenties, I had pretty massive debt which at first sort of overwhelmed me. Then I started practising and had to get loans to purchase all of my equipment and so on. But I remember reading an article in a magazine that depicted the lives of about five women at different stages with different financial circumstances. It included a twenty-six year old teacher who already owned her own home. It was a lovely little home. It wasn't elaborate but she had equity. I thought, "How does anybody do that?" What I learned from that article is even though you are in debt, you can always shave something off. You can organize your debt so that you are living up to your responsibility and satisfying your banker or whoever it is you borrowed money from, but still be saving a little bit for you.

At first I felt so obligated to pay back all my loans that I had barely ten cents left over to go to the grocery store and buy an orange. Well, of course I had to pay my loans and I did, but I found I could re-distribute whatever income I had so that I could put a little aside. I was also going out with a man who was a foreign exchange trader for a major bank, and he was the one who said, "What are you living so frantically for? Pay yourself first." He suggested that the first thing I did whenever I got a cheque was to take a certain amount and throw it into an account I didn't even look at – I needed to forget about it, he said. "But then when you want to go on a small holiday, you don't have to go into debt, its there. If you want to save for something, it's there."

I also had a girlfriend who at the time was teaching accounting at the faculty of management and she was appalled that I didn't have any knowledge about constructive borrowing. She said, at that time, there was something called an RHOSP, a Registered Home Ownership Savings Plan. I'm dating myself because I don't think they exist now. You could put aside $1,000 per year for 10 years. Well, I didn't have $1,000 as I was just out of school. She said, "If you don't go to the bank and borrow $1,000 now for the

Home Ownership plan and another $1,000 for your retirement plan I'll never speak to you again."

So, under the threat of losing her friendship, I went to the bank thinking they are never going to lend me more money. I had started my practice and I was amazed, the bank wanted to shove money at me. They knew they could basically mortgage my career. I said, "But I have to pay all of this back." They were willing to give me more than I was asking for and my banker made a pun. He said, "You mean you're refusing my advances?" I went back and called my girlfriend and said, "I don't know which it is, I'm either $2,000 richer or poorer. I'm not sure." She showed me how by even adding on to my existing debt, it was still cheaper to take advantage of these plans.

It was like forced savings. By the time I went to buy my first home, I was very grateful to have $10,000 plus interest to put down as a deposit. It was like magic to think that somebody like me could actually accumulate some money. It was like a miracle. That is how I started my retirement savings too; I realized that's how everyone does it. So I started up a bunch of little accounts. One of them was for a home and one was for retirement and one was for taxes. Originally, my accountant told me that in many ways I was shockingly disorganized financially, as doctors are known to be, but I learned. I think that too is part of the immigrant experience, you really do have a fear of being at the bottom and having to scrounge and make do all the time.

You have a nephew named Colin and you collect something called "Colin pennies."

Thank you for reminding me of that, you remember my little bits of history. I have a nephew who is now eleven and too smart for his own good. He is one of the lights of my life.

73

You know how you see pennies or nickels on the street, well when he was born I thought *I wonder what would happen if I started collecting them, what would they add up to?* I called them "Colin pennies" and I still collect them. Well, that kid now has a GIC of over $600 and more than $250 in an investment account. Not bad, and it's just a collection of pennies which Auntie tops up sometimes.

One day, you may give Colin this book. What would you like to tell him? What would you like him to know?

I would like him to know now, at age eleven, that you divide up your allowance, and you give a certain amount to charity every week. I believe that one should tithe oneself, even for a child if that means 25 cents a week. Put it aside for charity and I would say take off a similar amount and put it in a little piggy bank, then the rest goes in the bank. It's diligence and you get into the habit of always saving something. I would tell him that right now. As a matter of fact I've already given him little books on what kids can do to protect themselves financially. I would want him to have his own account that he opens himself and monitors.

I would also want him to get a rudimentary knowledge of the stock market, and an understanding of how things affect the world financially. To understand this very weird correlation: that the temperature in India sometimes does affect the sale of ice cream in North America because of the trade winds. That we really do buy more ice cream when we get hotter! That factors in certain parts of the world affect the economy and how people live in other parts of the world. I've never been wise enough to fully understand this myself, but I'd like him to.

At the same time, because I want his own life to be meaningful, I wouldn't say "Well just go into the stock market because that's how you're going to get more money." I don't think that's the point. The point is that he, by habit, knows how to take care of himself financially, just like you brush your teeth and take care of your health. There are some financial basics, some fundamentals. You wouldn't consider not brushing your teeth. You wouldn't consider not managing your finances even at the age of eleven.

Chapter Nine

Choices & Rewards

"My financial success is more important to me than anyone else's temporary discomfort, including my own."

anonymous

We sure dislike discomfort. We'll do just about anything to avoid discomfort, disappointment, pain, even hard work. We'll skirt around issues. We'll look for the most pain-free way to solve problems. We'll try different weight loss schemes or pills, including 'exercise in a bottle' rather than take the time and make the effort (consistently, day in day out, year in year out) to come by our results honestly. I know. Going for a run is one of the best things I can do for myself, the benefits for me far outweigh the effort, but the effort to get out the door is Herculean most times.

We'd rather spend $10 a week on lottery tickets than deposit $10 into our retirement savings plan on a weekly basis. Instead of thinking "no pain no gain" we think "no pain no pain." We are very good at avoiding challenging alternatives. Television is a great distraction. We avoid addressing our finances by watching TV. We avoid exercising by watching TV. We avoid shopping for and preparing healthy meals by watching TV, and as a result we resort to constant snacking. Some TV watching makes us better, more knowledgeable and understanding human beings. But for all the times I watch a program like "The Passionate Eye" on CBC, or a show which is funny and truly entertaining, I probably spend twice as much time channel surfing and watching what's on because it means I don't have to do or think about anything else. Channel surfing is less painful and takes a whole lot less effort.

What I'm finally beginning to understand, is that all choices are equally real. In a sense they are equally balanced or equally weighted. We create our own reality. The choice to watch television or go for a run is a real choice. I can say I'm going to do either one and whichever I do becomes my reality. However one option requires more effort to carry-out than the other, and that's the key. In order to preserve my integrity, in order to lessen my stress level and take ownership of my life, not only do I need to look after my health by going for a run, I also need to be conscious of the decisions I am making. If my default position is to flop down in front of the TV then I can't deny I've made a choice. And along with free will and the ability to choose our activities comes the ability to choose our attitude. Acknowledging responsibility for one's own attitude can be a harder pill to swallow.

It's true for financial planning. It's as easy to spend $10 on your retirement plan as it is to spend $10 on anything else, including impulse purchases, such as a lottery ticket. Ten dollars is ten dollars; it's the same $10. But one choice requires more effort to carry out than the other. The lottery ticket is "no pain and potential gain in the neighbourhood of 14 million to one" while the retirement plan contribution is "consistent short-term pain for future long-term gain with much better odds."

Let's acknowledge that sometimes the best financial choices can be painful to make, but always remind ourselves that both the immediate sense of satisfaction and the potential for long-term gain far outweigh our temporary discomfort. Rather than focussing on the 20% of financial planning which is very challenging, let's focus on the 80% which is rewarding, both emotionally and monetarily.

"Never grow a wishbone, daughter, where your backbone ought to be."

Clementine Paddleford, American journalist

There is a government-sponsored series of TV commercials which I find offensive because they promote gambling as opposed to working, saving and investing wisely. Make no mistake about it, lotteries are a classic form of gambling including those where the money goes to a good cause. If you purchase lottery tickets and rationalize your purchase by thinking, "Well at least the money helps a well-known charity, a local childrens' hospital or a seniors' group," don't think you are not gambling. If it was really important to you to support those causes you would make charitable donations, and perhaps you do. But when you buy lottery tickets, you're gambling. The irony of the TV commercials is their promotion of the same message that is in this book: Freedom … Just Imagine.

Just imagine if you were healthy and had no financial worries. What a lovely exercise: sit back, close your eyes and imagine the freedom. Who would you be? What would you do? Just imagine what you could accomplish on a micro level, how you would live day-to-day, and on a macro level, what you could accomplish out in the world.

How would you spend your days if you were healthy and energetic with no reason to worry financially? What if you didn't have to work as long and as hard as you do? What if you could choose to work part-time or not at all? Would you spend more time with your family, your children, parents, grandchildren, nieces or nephews? What about your spouse or partner – how would you spend more time with him or her? Who would you like to see more often? Maybe you'd grab a friend and take cruises around the world or maybe, what you would really like to do, is take a parent or elderly grandparent out for a leisurely lunch every week. Maybe you would like to read bedtime stories to little ones without being exhausted and short-tempered. Maybe you would do everything you are doing now when you're not at work, but you would have the time to do it and you'd be relaxed. As a result of not being pre-occupied with current or future financial worries, you could enjoy each moment of every activity which brings you bliss. Of course, more time spent with wonderful, dear friends near or far away would be at the top of all our lists.

Perhaps you are one of those smart people who has discovered what you love to do and you're already doing it. If you love your work but you are not currently independently wealthy, imagine being able to pursue your occupation without having to worry about job security, performance appraisals and salary reviews, maintaining your benefit coverage or moving up the corporate ladder. Freedom ... Just Imagine.

And think about your life on a macro level. At the end of the day, when we die, we want to think that in some way the world has been a better place because we were here. If you were financially secure, how would you assist the world? How would the rest of us know what you had done and the examples you had set? It's not a question of celebrity or fame, it's a question of character and reputation. As a kid on overnight canoe trips we were taught to leave the campsite cleaner than we found it. Imagine that on a macro level. How would you leave this world in a cleaner, more whole and peaceful state?

Would you volunteer? Are there non-profit organizations which you feel play an incredibly important role? Would you like to participate in their work, perhaps at the local level or maybe at the international level? I would want to know that in some way I assisted in preserving the diversity of flora and fauna on this planet as opposed to destroying it. I would spend part of my day picking up garbage in greenbelts and creeks, just as I did when I was a kid with my friend Carey. Carey had to walk her dog Brownie every morning before school and I would keep her company. We grew up on the same street with a ravine behind our houses. We would walk Brownie while picking-up garbage in the ravine because we knew it was good for the environment. It was fun and we thought, even back then, it was the right thing to do. Never underestimate a kid's ability to think and act!

Here's another thought, you and I can read this book or any other book we choose and mull over the ideas it contains. We can get on our computer and type a message to a friend a mile away or thousands of miles away and say, "I just came across a neat article and it made me think of you." In my mind, the greatest invention of the 20th century was flight, but that has to be followed pretty closely by e-mail. When my grandmothers left Great Britain in the 1920's they left everyone behind. Letters took weeks and they didn't know if or when they would see their families again. No one has to be in that position today. If you know someone in Australia, Bulgaria, Chile or Denmark you can communicate with him or her via e-mail faster than you can make a cup of coffee. But you and I can only do that because of literacy. Imagine being illiterate in this world? How isolating and terrifying that would be. You would feel like a second-class citizen and you could easily be taken advantage of. So when we go back to thinking about what we could accomplish on a macro-level, if we didn't need to be focussed on our own financial circumstances, perhaps one of our goals would be to help eradicate illiteracy in the world. To ensure that there is an equal standard of education for all children and adults, especially for those who have fallen through the cracks.

Freedom ... Just Imagine. That's the tag-line which is used to get us to buy lottery tickets but what if we turned it around and used it as the slogan to empower us as individuals? What if we put that slogan on the bulletin board above our desks, on our bedside table, inside our kitchen cupboards, on a mini post-it note stuck to each credit card? And every time we read it, it inspired us to take action as individuals to secure our own freedom. What if it empowered us to do financial planning or pursue financial wisdom? What if it empowered us to become self-sufficient, healthy, wealthy and wise? What if ... Just imagine.

"I don't know anything about luck. I've never banked on it, and I'm afraid of people who do. Luck to me is something else: hard work - and realizing what is opportunity and what isn't."

Lucille Ball, American actress

The tag-line "Freedom ... Just imagine" leads my thinking in another direction too. Nobody enjoys visualizing complete and everlasting financial freedom more than I do, but the truth is, that may not be a very realistic goal. I don't want to waste precious hours and energy pursuing one unwieldy, out-of-proportion, over-the-top dream. And as much as I would love to be wealthy, wealthy, wealthy beyond belief, it would be a sad state of affairs if I truly thought my life wasn't successful nor had meaning unless I'd achieved that material state of being. I am not a driven, competitive, obsessed person by nature. It's not important to me to be a mover and a shaker, an over-achiever, always at the top of my game, the king of the castle. Those characteristics are very useful when you are trying to acquire wealth. And we all need them to some degree. Having no ambition would equate to making no improvements in our lives at all. But if my only goal is the largest net worth I can imagine and I don't reach my own outlandish expectations, then I will have wasted a lot of time and energy that could have been better spent making a difference in the present.

While it is empowering and enjoyable to be inspired and while it is satisfying to work hard for achievable goals, it doesn't make sense to have an obsession for wealth that is completely impractical. What's at stake is our sanity. Sometimes we need to drop our desired standard of living a notch in order to improve our quality of life. Or at the very least, we need to review our expectations and focus our energy on contentment as well as financial independence.

To be content doesn't imply settling or being unmotivated. And it certainly isn't laziness. Contentment comes with time and maturity; it is closely associated to wisdom. My older clients who are in a more precarious position financially and who don't have the ability to earn income in the workforce are often more content than my clients in their thirties and forties who are striving to do it all and have it all. Contentment is not resignation. Contentment is discerning: it is a decision which then becomes an attitude of ease and acceptance. Some of us choose contentment sooner than others. Grandma Duncan used to say (and I believe it was her grandmother who passed down this golden nugget) "You can't put an old head on young shoulders." We all get to experience life and learn from it. Each of us will learn many of the same lessons at different times. And each generation will learn its own lessons. Wisdom comes with age *and* with reflection.

What changes would you like to make to your standard of living today, so that you could have a better quality of life now and in the future? Or as a dear friend who is 56 said to me: "I know I won't be rich. It's too late for me now. But I choose to be smart."

We can choose to look at various options. We can choose to be resourceful. And it's never too late to be smart.

"For me success isn't about living up to others' expectations. It's about feeling comfortable with what I achieve."
An advertisement for *Mark's Work Wearhouse*

Chapter Ten

Caroline M.

Caroline is a 34 year old pharmacist who recently become engaged. Caroline's parents were born in China, she and her siblings were born in Canada.

Caroline, how did you decide to do so much traveling?

I think it was just after I finished my internship. After all those years of school, I thought I would like to get away. I went with a friend from my Pharmacy class in October of 1990 for three months. We saw Australia, New Zealand, Fiji and Hawaii.

That first big trip we did was organized. My friend had a travel agent who'd arranged everything. All of our tours were booked beforehand and we knew exactly which hotels we were staying at. My friend was gung-ho and followed the itinerary to a "T." She kind of drove me crazy but we're still friends today. There wasn't really anything about that trip that was spontaneous.

The next time I went traveling it was to Europe for five months with the guy I was seeing at the time. That trip was more rugged. We rented a car for part of it and we camped a lot. At this point I was getting into traveling, but I still wasn't sure I could do it by myself.

When you went into Pharmacy, did you know to what extent that profession was going to allow you to travel?

Up until the end of high school you think, "I still have another year, I can decide next year." Then all of a sudden you have to fill out a university application and decide what to do. I had no idea. My parents had a Chinese friend and she was a pharmacist. They said, "Susan's a pharmacist. Why don't you be a pharmacist?" I didn't have any other ideas and I thought "well, OK." It was a pretty hard program to get into. I thought, I'll write the exam and if I get in, good and if I don't, I don't. Basically in high school you were told that to get into any program, you had to have your maths and sciences. I took all of my sciences even though I hated physics and I wasn't big on biology. And I took all of my maths which I didn't really enjoy, but I didn't find them hard either.

Now I have been working as a pharmacist, when I'm not traveling, for ten years. There is a shortage of pharmacists, which is good for me because it has allowed me to take breaks to travel and then come back to work. When I came back from Australia, I started working, paid off my student debt, bought a car and paid it off too.

I went to Africa by myself for six months. Those six months turned into seven when I got stuck in Ghana. Originally, I wanted to go for a year but I couldn't get a one-year, open ticket. The travel agency said they could get me a six-month ticket but I had to choose a city to fly into and a city to fly out of. I chose to fly into Johannesberg, then I looked at the map of Africa. Did I want to travel the east coast or west coast? I decided I'd go to Casablanca. Between Johannesberg, and Casablanca my trip was unplanned. I bought a *Lonely Planet* guide book and took it with me.

When I traveled to Asia and India I bought a ticket with Singapore Airlines that allowed me a number of stopovers. That ticket was open for a year and I could come back early if I wanted to. In fact I probably could have stayed longer but

I was looking forward to coming home after being in India for five months - it's a pretty hard country in which to travel. Luckily, a friend of mine I had met while I was in Africa, (she lives in Australia) agreed to meet up with me on this trip. It was easier when the two of us were traveling together. We were backpacking it. We had a really good time and I would do it again.

Financially you've been able to buy a condominium and now you're planning to get married. What did your family or your background teach you about money?

My parents worked really hard. They didn't spend a lot of money on themselves. We didn't live a rich lifestyle, we had basic things. I remember going on one trip in my whole childhood. No, I think we went on two trips. We went to visit my grandfather when he was alive in Mexico and that was a big family vacation.

My parents worked continuously in the restaurant they owned and didn't take holidays. It was closed on Sundays, but my Dad had to do the paperwork. He would be at the restaurant all Sunday doing paperwork, then we would go and meet him and he would make us dinner.

I remember on Sunday nights we sorted out the money from the restaurant on my parents' bed. It was our job to put all the one dollar bills together, all the five's together and all the 10's & 20's. That was a big job to us as kids and we handled money at a young age. It wasn't for play that we were doing this, I knew it had to be counted properly and kept in piles. I would also help my Dad with his accounting ledgers which I didn't really understand, but he would tell me where to write down the amounts.

We used to invest in Canada Savings Bonds. My Dad would say "Oh, it's a good year this year" so we would take out whatever money we had in our piggy bank and buy a $100 bond. It meant we got a piece of paper, and never saw it again since Dad took it from us and put it in a safety deposit box. Then about ten years later when it matured, he would say, "Here you go, here's your money." We'd think, wow, I had forgotten all about this!

We had bank accounts but we didn't have an allowance. We really never asked for anything either. We saved because we lived in a small town and there wasn't a lot for us to spend our money on. There were things that we could do for free, and for those things which required money such as swimming lessons, we weren't aware of how much it cost our parents. And it didn't cost any money to take books out of the library, unless your books were late then it was 3 cents a book a day. We were allowed to borrow six books at one time and we only lived one block away. We would take out six books, go home and read them all, then go back the next day to get another six books. This was normal for our family. We just loved reading.

Your parents weren't in the medical profession, but you are a pharmacist, your brothers are doctors and your sister is completing her doctorate in psychiatry. You are all very accomplished.

I don't know if we always thought we were going to be doctors. I think only in the end did my youngest brother feel he had to be in the medical field instead of going into business because the older ones had set the trail.

Financially, if you look over the last ten years is there anything you would have done differently?

Not really. I have spent a lot of money traveling, but I did a lot of things while I was away so I feel I got my money's worth. I don't think that I would have made any big changes. I bought an expensive car, and everyone says when you drive it off the lot it loses half of it's value, but I really like the car and its comfortable. It's a 1992 Toyota and I still drive it although it was probably in storage for a total of three and a half years while I traveled.

It's amazing that you lucked into your career, because it doesn't sound like there was much planning involved. There is a shortage of people doing your job and it is not 9 to 5. Its shift work and you can work extra shifts and take a month off and come back.

I sort of knew this when I got into pharmacy, because that was one of the selling features of the profession. Well, I didn't think of it as a selling feature at the time when my Mom said, "Why don't you go into pharmacy because then you can have a family and you can work as well." Some people do it part-time. The college dictates that we have to work 600 hours in a three year time frame to maintain our license. So that's what I did when I was gone for two years, I just made up the hours within the next three years and it wasn't hard. There are pharmacies open 24 hours a day.

Has debt ever been a problem for you?

No, I've been really fortunate that way. I've never bought anything that I didn't think I could pay off right away. Even when I bought the appliances for my new condo on my credit card I knew I could pay for them. I wouldn't have gone away on my trips if I didn't have the money.

I decided to go from renting to owning a condo because I was getting sick and tired of paying rent. I didn't especially love the brown walls in my apartment or the lilac tub & toilet and the shag carpeting. I wanted to have my own place where I could do my own thing. When you change someone else's wall colouring it's not really something you're doing for yourself. It's still someone else's wall.

I wasn't sure I wanted to buy a house because there's a lot of maintenance. And I also thought "do I want to pay condo fees?" Then this loft came up. It was close to where I was living and I really liked the location. I thought I'd come and take a look, and I bought it. When I was signing the papers it occurred to me "What am I doing? This is a lot of money." It was a huge step and then my fear was "this is really tying me down too. I can't just pack up and take off, now I have to worry about things." But it means I have permanent storage. When I was renting and I wanted to travel for a long period I would have to put everything in storage and I dread the thought of moving my belongings again.

So now I have a mortgage but my mortgage is less than my rent was. I still feel somewhat tied down. I suppose I could rent it out. And I suppose if I really wanted to I could just turn around and sell it, although I am kind of attached to it. It's starting to feel like home. It's even going to be hard when I move to the city where my fiancé lives. Tim and I haven't decided what we're going to do.

How did you meet Tim?

It's a funny story. A couple of years ago I was sick and tired of winter and thought I would just buy a ticket and go somewhere warm. Actually I was thinking of backpacking in Cuba. On *The Lonely Planet* website there's a section for traveling companions. He had written that he was looking for a travel companion to go to Honduras. I e-mailed him and said "I don't know if you are aware but Hurricane Mitch has gone through and blown the country apart so as a result there is not a whole lot to do there!" I didn't know if he had just picked a place; thrown a dart and decided he was going to Honduras.

I said if he wasn't fully committed to Honduras, would he consider going to Cuba? As it turned out he had booked his trip months before and he was going to do scuba diving. I ended up going to Mexico instead because I got a really good deal on airfare. We just kept e-mailing back and forth about traveling and stuff, but normally when you e-mail it's to share ideas and that's often the end of it. I thought well, I'm going on my trip and he's going on his and we'll lose touch.

When I got back home he had sent me a "welcome back" e-mail which I thought was very sweet. Then, probably a week later while he was still away on his trip I got another e-mail. I had just worked a twelve hour day plus an hour of driving in a snowstorm and I was crabby. In his e-mail he wanted me to call Air Canada and confirm his flight because the communication in Honduras was very poor and unreliable. He also wanted to make sure he had his free upgrade from economy to business class. I'm thinking, "No, you suffer, you sit back with the cattle." I also thought, "I don't even know this guy."

I called Air Canada and little did I know I was going to be on hold for what seemed like two hours. I wasn't using my cordless phone, so I was stuck to my phone because you know you're going to be the next person they answer. I'm waiting and I'm waiting to confirm this guy's flight that I don't know. I thought, "Why am I doing this? I'm tired, I've just come home and it's eleven o'clock at night. Doesn't he have a mother who can do this for him?" He figured because I was such a savvy traveler I would understand about confirming flights, but little did he know that I had never ever confirmed a flight. If this is the date and time on my ticket then that's when I go to the airport. I've never called to see if my flight has been delayed or cancelled. So the first time I confirm a flight in my whole life it's not even for me.

That's how it happened. We just kept talking back and forth after that, and one day we decided we were going to meet. I made trips from Ottawa to Burlington where my parents had moved and he lived in St. Catharine's. We decided we'd meet halfway. He was really poor with directions. He was nervous and he got up early in the morning to wash his car and to make me these cookies on sticks. He decided he didn't want to give me flowers because it was warm and he was afraid they would die in the car. His mother wanted to know what the hell he was doing in the kitchen. He was baking chocolate chip cookies, using heart-shaped cookie cutters and putting them on sticks.

Now you're engaged and you live in two different cities, is this going to change your financial planning?

Financially, I don't know what kind of impact marriage is going to have. I make more money than Tim does. Actually we've talked about money a little bit and what we're going to do about bank accounts and things like that. He's not a big spender. He wants nice things too, but he's happy to save for them. He's bought property on which to build a house. We may build the house in such a way that it has a complete apartment downstairs that we can rent to pay the mortgage. I will still have payments on my condo, unless I decide I want to sell it. So there will be some financial changes.

We've talked about retirement which consisted of Tim saying that if he won a million dollars he'd pay for my ticket and he'd take me with him to Borneo where we'd do volunteer work at the orangutan camp. He hates the fact that I've been to

Borneo and he hasn't. That was one of the reasons we kept in contact, I was going to give him tips on what to do in Borneo. We haven't gone yet.

Last year you became an aunt. What would you tell your niece, Kate?

Get an education. That's my biggest piece of advice. We never thought about not going to school. When we were in high school my parents banned us from going to school dances. My mother thought that if my sister and I went we would come home, become single unwed mothers, go on welfare and not go back to school. My mother really thought that's what happens if you go to school dances.

We always had marks in the 90's. One year I was forced to take gym because it was part of our high school curriculum. We had to have so many credits in each category and I picked gym. I cried when I got my mark because it was 65. I was really bad, I couldn't play basketball, I couldn't do anything. I was so upset because it pulled my average down. My saving grace was that in the second term of gym we had two health units that I could actually study for, so I redeemed myself there. But my brothers, my sister and I studied all the time.

I shared a tiny room with my sister and we had bunk beds. I thought that was so unfair because both of our brothers had their own rooms. We were the oldest and we had to share. We had a little desk in there but I only used it as a spring board to get onto my bed. We'd either do our homework at the coffee table in the living room or we sat in the kitchen. We lived in a really old house. Usually I remember sitting in the drafty kitchen doing homework by myself and everyone else sat at the coffee table in front of the TV. My parents never told us we couldn't watch TV. We got our homework done and our grades showed it.

It's interesting that your one piece of financial advice to baby Kate is to get an education. An education gives you the potential for options. Without an education you're at the mercy of everyone else in the market.

It's really important. Oftentimes you are taking courses and thinking, "Where's this going to lead me?" I've found that employers are more likely to hire someone with an education even if the job doesn't require that education. Their perspective is: this person persevered and went through school so I know they have dedication and they have the capacity to try to learn new things.

Do you worry about your parents outliving their savings?

No one really talks about it. I don't know my parents' financial situation. I know they never had a lot of money and whatever money they had, they put towards us. They didn't have much money for our education. We received student assistance from the government based on our parents' income and when I was in university I worked part-time plus I had my job in the summer. My parents helped us out but not directly with money.

We would come home from university and they would send us back with food: Chicken fingers in tin foil, lasagna and shepherd's pie all wrapped in a box. I would be carrying this huge box first on the bus (with all my books too) then on the subway, and when I got back to the apartment I shared with three other girls, I'd have to explain that I was sorry but I needed ALL the space in the freezer.

My parents looked out for us that way. Now that they're retired my Dad plays the stock market but they live within their means. They say they don't need a whole lot. After we went away to various universities they chose to move to Burlington where my Dad's brother lives and where they could be closer to us in case something happened. They may be thinking about a retirement home. My Dad probably thinks he's going to pass away first and then my mother would be able to look after herself in a home. They shouldn't ever have to worry about money because there are four of us who would provide for them.

I don't think we've come right out and talked about supporting our parents down the road. Within the Chinese culture it was understood that the parents would always stay with the oldest son, but because we're here in Canada values change, times change and people live longer. Tim has even said when we move into our house, if my parents want to live in the basement apartment, that's OK. I thought it was really nice of him to make the offer. I don't think my parents have a lot of money but they don't need anything. All they really want is to have the kids come home and visit. Anytime there is a big holiday, my mom gets upset if we can't all get home.

What have been some of your best and worst financial decisions?

Some of my best financial decisions: I look back and think that I made a good choice in buying this loft, because of the real estate market right now. I'm sure it's gone up in value.

Some of my worst decisions: I might have made some bad mutual fund choices but I haven't studied my funds that much to really dwell on it. I know a lot of things go in cycles anyway. Maybe if I look back and I have had a fund for 20 years and it's really made nothing, then I might say that was a bad idea or choice. But I look at the bottom line of all my funds to see the total amount and that's what I base it on.

I heard something recently on the radio while I was driving. The commentator said that part of the increasing cost of health care is because we are now being diagnosed and treated for things we used to live with before, and he gave the example of Viagra. There may be conditions that we human beings had in the past and we learned to accept, but not anymore.

We're a lot more aware, it's true. I went to a good continuing education session yesterday on womens' health. They talked about how PMS was never considered a disorder. Now it is identified. Before people just thought you were crazy if you were complaining about all these problems. We talked about the different issues that weren't addressed 30 years ago, for example menopause. It was very interesting.

I think we have a really good health care system here. It's true there are a lot more disease conditions than there were 30 or 40 years ago. There are more 'disease states' for example AIDS where people can stay alive but the drugs which keep them alive are expensive. Transplants are another example where individuals now survive these procedures but it requires drugs to maintain their life. Also they are developing drugs to treat and slow down Alzheimer's. Our job as a pharmacist will always be there.

I'm glad you're there Caroline, thank you.

Chapter Eleven

Financial Planning & Different Personalities

> "Your happiness is intertwined
> with your outlook on life."
>
> Chinese fortune cookie

Now we are at the nuts & bolts stage of this book. What is financial planning? It is the time you set aside to reflect upon your existing financial situation, to decide where you would like to be headed, and then to decide how best you can make changes to get there. A plan is not carved in stone. It's just that, a plan, and it considers your current circumstances and knowledge. Remember, your knowledge will increase and your circumstances will change. As a result you will improve upon and revise your financial plan as life progresses.

This is an activity you can do alone, or with a partner if there is a person in your life with whom you are financially entwined. However, I suggest that you start the process by yourself so that you are clear about what is important to you and what you are willing to do to achieve your goals with or without a partner. It is rare that partners are totally in synch every step of the way in the planning process. Listed below are some of my experiences when it comes to partners, usually a husband and wife relationship, although it could include other combinations such as a parent and adult child:

1. The partners acknowledge their differences. They've come to accept that one finds the job of managing finances more satisfying than the other. The one who finds it least interesting will listen however, and be part of the decision making process, because he or she knows it is too important a subject to ignore.

2. The partners may have come to realize they are opposites. One is a saver and the other is a spender. Or they have very different comfort levels when it comes to investing. With the saver/spender combination, the spender usually acknowledges that the two of them wouldn't have any kind of a nest egg if it weren't for the other. When I'm sitting down with this couple it is the spender's indirect way of publicly thanking the saver for having stood his or her ground. Where two people have very different comfort levels regarding types of investments or how to invest, this needs to be respected and each should have their own portfolio. Their joint portfolio should be a compromise (in the good sense of the word) between their investment styles.

3. I may find I'm sitting down with partners who are still discovering how different they are. They're either partially dismayed by their differences or they haven't figured out a way to get ahead financially while working around the other. This is a harder scenario because I am having to read between the lines and trying to interpret the dynamics: how did these two people make decisions in the past separately and how likely are they to be able to compromise and stick with or work through a new plan in the future? This couple doesn't understand why they can't get along financially and why the other doesn't see things as they do. The financial planning process is tougher for these two, but that may be one of the reasons

I've been called in. They need a third party to act as the coach and to encourage them as a team. I reassure them that the norm is two people don't think and act alike all the time, especially when it involves money. They are grateful that someone understands their different patterns and will help them incorporate this into a workable plan.

4. The rarer combination is two peas in a pod. When I'm working with a couple who are completely in synch regarding the importance of saving and investing; how much, where and when; who understand the significance of having their wills and powers of attorney updated, knowing who will be the executors, guardians and beneficiaries; who appreciate the value of being adequately insured; a couple who isn't afraid to look at the financial consequences of living a long life or of outliving the other, then my job is so much easier. This is definitely the rarer scenario.

5. A combination which frightens me is where a couple has fallen into the pattern of one partner having all the knowledge and management of the finances for both. The party who has acquiesced may have done so for a number of reasons. A) He or she thinks highly of the managing partner whom they feel has done a very good job at looking after everything. B) He or she may not want to make the effort to be financially responsible and is happy to pass it off to the other who seems more interested or willing. C) One party has grown tired of asking questions of the other in order to understand his or her partner's financial circumstances, and to be allowed to have an equal say in how money is spent and saved. The demanding party has let up because to pursue their demands for access to information and an equal voice was ultimately jeopardizing the relationship. This person has chosen the current structure of the

relationship first, and secondly is hoping for the best financially. D) Because of culture or family history, the silent partner feels it is the responsibility of the other to manage the finances and therefore both their financial futures. To suggest otherwise would diminish the role of the managing partner. The silent partner believes they are being respectful. This view, however, is no longer realistic or practical. I still have female clients who did not know how to write a cheque until their husbands became ill. They had to learn a lot and quickly which put them at a disadvantage and added to their distress at a time when they needed to be strong and coping well.

Regarding scenario "A" above, where one partner has done an excellent job managing all aspects of the couple's finances, the silent partner should still be cognizant of what has been accomplished and how.

When I went to see a retired couple concerning the renewal of a small investment the wife owned, I asked questions about this particular investment and how it fit into the overall portfolio. I was comfortable with the answers I received: the overall portfolio was balanced and diversified. The only problem was that as soon as I walked into the house the wife told me I would be dealing with her husband because he handled the finances, even though the investment was in her name. Indeed that was the case, the husband had handled all their investments through fifty years of marriage. He was educated and well-informed, and he'd managed very well. I began asking the wife a few questions to find out if she understood what her husband had done, if she truly understood the investments which she could inherit.

Her husband was in his late seventies and she was a few years younger. I remember she was in the living room with us, but I had the impression she was staying to be polite. She was a lovely lady, however I'm sure if it hadn't seemed rude she would have gone off to another part of the house to enjoy her own activities while we discussed financial planning. She told me she wasn't worried because her husband and son talked on the phone often, including talks about investments, so if something happened she knew their son could manage the investing her husband had started. This disturbed me because the son lived in another province and was a three hour plane ride away. I'm sure he had a job and maybe a family of his own. If she didn't understand their holdings, which were many, she would need her son to be hands-on when her husband died.

6. If neither partner has given any thought to financial planning or if they feel they are invincible; if they haven't considered the reality of their future and they are only interested in spending and acquiring, probably getting into debt in the process (euphemistically called "buying on credit"), chances are they don't know I exist. And the truth is that until they begin to manage their debt and start learning to live within their means, there is little I can do. As a financial planner I don't have a magic wand which will produce more money, a better paying job or a higher level of education. I certainly can't make consumer debt vanish with a snap of the fingers. Unfortunately I've met people I cannot assist because they need debt counseling before they need to meet with a Certified Financial Planner.

So if you fear that your partner may not value the need to do financial planning as much as you do, or may not be encouraging your desire to become financially savvy and secure, don't let that dissuade you from looking after yourself. You wouldn't let someone stop you from trying to live a healthier life, eating nutritious food and getting your work-outs in.   In fact, your partner may jump on the bandwagon at a later date.   My husband didn't recycle anything when I met him, now every scrap of paper goes into the black box and our blue box is overflowing. Sometimes they learn!

"At the time you conceive the result you want, the actual way you will bring it about is always unknown to you, even if you have a hunch about it."

Robert Fritz, *The Path of Least Resistance*

Chapter Twelve

Working with a CFP

> "If you could have a housekeeper, a personal trainer or a financial planner, which would you choose? Choose the financial planner because she'll show you how to have the other two."
>
> Heather Duncan, CFP

Now lets look at what a financial planner does and why you might want to consider working with one. There is a reason the job exists. When it comes to managing money and building wealth, it's a lot more complicated than it used to be. A Certified Financial Planner (CFP) will help you focus on what you can control and manage. More than managing clients' money, we try to help clients manage their behaviour and expectations around their money. We try to influence clients' perception of money in all its different forms: as income, debt, investments, taxes, inheritance, insurance premiums and benefits, etc. As a CFP, my goal is that each client has a balanced perspective to match his or her balanced portfolio.

A financial planner acts like a personal trainer for one's finances. Think of all the reasons you would go to a personal trainer. Maybe you want to increase your overall health, lose some weight or get rid of some bad habits. Maybe you know what you need to do but you want someone to help you stay on track, someone who will appreciate your challenges, who believes in you and will encourage you. Maybe you have a specific goal such as running a marathon one day. Maybe you don't know anything about exercise equipment, and you need someone who is knowledgeable to show you what equipment you should be using. Maybe a family member developed osteoporosis, heart disease, or diabetes and you want to avoid the same outcome.

These are all legitimate reasons to seek out the services of a Certified Personal Trainer and there are equivalent reasons for doing the same with a Certified Financial Planner. Maybe you want to increase your overall wealth, to grow your net worth. Maybe you want to reduce your debt and get out of the bad habit of buying lottery tickets instead of investing in your retirement plan. Maybe you've previously read books or articles on financial planning and you actually know what you need to do, but you'd like to have a professional partner who will help you follow through on the necessary steps. Maybe you have a specific goal such as retiring as a millionaire one day. Maybe you don't know anything about financial planning, you don't know the difference between a bond and a stock, and you'd like someone to answer your questions and provide helpful explanations. Maybe you have a family member who outlived their savings and became dependent on others or dependent on the government; or you know friends who became disabled or critically ill and it affected not only them, but also those who depended on them and you don't want to experience the same fate. These are all good reasons to work with a CFP.

None of us can abdicate responsibility for ourselves. We are each accountable for how we live. We cannot farm out our responsibility for our health – mental, physical or emotional. We can't outsource our material responsibilities.

In our own lives we must practice stewardship, leadership and management. We can choose to increase our net worth and we can also choose to live appreciatively, conserving natural resources and being respectful of the rights and needs of others. However, that is a lot to look after in an average day. So we turn to others. We efficiently make use of the knowledge and experience of those who've gone before us, especially those who've worked and studied in an area we want to improve upon. Really, we each need to be our own financial planner just as we need to be our own nutritionist, physician, psychologist, judge, advocate, friend, teacher, mentor and at times, our own fairy godmother. But it makes sense to get guidance where we can and especially when we need it. It pays to seek out wisdom.

When it comes to managing material resources, have you thought about how much money you, as an individual, will administer in your lifetime? It's probably more than you realize especially if you are looking at your pay stub, and after deductions you think far too little goes into the bank. Here's a suggestion – add up the amount of money you've made every year since you started working (before deductions). You may have copies of your tax returns going back to your first working days and can easily look up your total income in each year. If not, you can do a ballpark calculation, i.e. "I probably averaged this amount annually in my early twenties, this amount in my mid-twenties, this much when I was thirty" etc. Now calculate how many more years you will keep working and multiply that number by what you think your average income could be. You want to get to **one final figure**, which says: over my entire lifetime this is how much money I will have earned.

Even if you do very general calculations I think your "worth" will floor you. Then consider how well you've spent, saved and invested that income. Do you want to make all the same money choices in the next 10, 20, 30 years as you did in the past? To take the exercise one step further, calculate all the income tax you've paid and will pay in your lifetime. Again, the final figure will be eye-opening. When I even begin to contemplate this exercise it makes me re-appreciate the value of every loonie & twoonie in my wallet. Every dollar you and I make, whether we keep it or spend it, is hard earned. And to not value that dollar in our pocket is to not value ourselves.

If you'd like guidance in managing your monetary resources, a CFP can help. A good financial planner will concentrate on what is important to you as an individual and together you will develop a plan to achieve your goals. A financial planner will help you weed out information that's not applicable, and will guide you through the maze of financial products and choices out there. He or she will make suitable recommendations and will pay attention to the investment, taxation and insurance considerations which are yours, not somebody else's. A CFP will help you to achieve your personal, financial goals by working within your means. We each have a mental picture of what our "ideal tomorrow" would look like, and we want to know that we have taken the best steps possible to get there.

When you meet with a CFP, what will he or she do? Here's an indication of what will happen in the first meeting and perhaps the second. (Your meetings could last from one to two hours.) This may not be the actual order the items are dealt with, but they should be addressed.

After the usual self-introductions, a CFP will ask why you wanted to meet. He or she will want to know what your concerns are, what triggered the initial get-together. You will be asked about your goals and dreams – what is important to you, what you would you like to accomplish. The planner will give you some background information about themselves, information on the company or companies the planner represents, and information on how he or she is compensated. There should be no obligation when you meet with a planner for the first time and if you have subsequent meetings, you will want to know how the CFP covers the cost of his or her time and experience.

The first meeting or two is not only one of introduction but also for data gathering. It is important to ask questions, and that you feel comfortable with how you are being received, that you feel there is rapport. Is this someone who seems to understand you, is listening and trying to provide you with relevant information? You could choose to work with this person for a number of reasons: their credentials, their experience, because they came highly recommended, because their firm has a good reputation. But at the end of the day, this will be a relationship based on trust.

Trust is earned and it cannot be fully earned in one sitting. I met with a prospective client, a young intern who would be a family doctor in a few months time. I was recommended to her by a good friend. I could tell as our meeting progressed that she wasn't entirely comfortable with the steps I was proposing. She was worried about where I would be putting her investments when we weren't at the investing stage yet. It would be months before we started investing as first we needed to build a cushion for her. I was pleased that she was asking questions but I was aware of the time. I felt that if I told her everything I'd want her to know and answered all her questions about financial planning at our first meeting, I would still be at the same chair in her dining-room two days later.

I hadn't earned her trust yet, and I didn't know if I could in the time scheduled for that first meeting. In the beginning, until we worked together longer, her trust would have to be an act of faith. I tried to reassure her. I explained that it was just as if I had come to see her as a family doctor. If I told her my throat was sore and she examined my throat and prescribed medicine or told me that perhaps I'd need to have my tonsils out, then on some level I would have to trust her: A) because I can't see inside my throat the way she can; I couldn't see what she was looking at, and B) because I'm not a doctor, I have no medical training. My prospective client was very kind, she said she understood the analogy, which made it easier to move forward in the planning.

If you are feeling comfortable, the meeting will continue and now the planner will be asking you all kinds of questions about your current financial circumstances; investments you've made in the past, what you own and what you owe, insurance you've purchased, who prepares your taxes, do you have a copy of last year's return, do you have a will and powers of attorney, who are your dependents or future dependents, etc. The more information you can provide the better the recommendations a CFP can offer.

After the planner has gathered all the information needed in that first meeting they will go away, review and analyze it, and want to meet with you again to discuss a preliminary plan. Before the CFP leaves you will probably both have an idea of the areas you will start working on first because you'll have discussed priorities. Further in this book there are a number of exercises which you can do to help prepare to meet with a CFP. And if you aren't working with an advisor, you'll want to complete the exercises to have a better understanding of your circumstances and to help you prepare your own plan of action.

In many jurisdictions people can legally call themselves financial advisors or even financial planners, so you will want to know the experience and the qualifications of the individual you are meeting. The designation CFP (Certified Financial Planner) is internationally recognized. Someone who has this designation has met a number of qualifications including standards of training, examination, experience, ethics and continuing education. The CFP trademark is designed to identify those holding a CFP license to the public. In Canada, a CFP is licensed by the Financial Planners Standards Council and must annually maintain his or her license by meeting the requirements of the Council. This is a not-for-profit, professional, regulatory organization and their website is: www.cfp-ca.org.

A CFP may have chosen to specialize in an area of planning or to work with a certain segment of the public. Don't hesitate to ask who would be a typical client for them. Think about what you would like from the relationship and express your expectations.

Going back to the idea that a financial planner is like a personal trainer for your finances, I want to point out another similarity. Just as a personal trainer can't do the abdominal crunches for you, a financial planner can't put money into your retirement plan for you. In other words, regardless of how good the plan is, it doesn't replace you, the participant. A good plan needs you to implement it; you will be the one who "works" the plan. Just as it's your body, at the end of the day, it's also your money.

Not deciding to plan for the future could be costly. And to plan is anything but selfish. It's very rare in life that we achieve goals without considering tactics for their achievement. If we have a goal or dream in mind then we subconsciously look for opportunities to make things happen and we seek out the information and knowledge we need. If we don't do some financial planning then we could miss out on realizing dreams which are very important to us like buying a home or saving for a child's university education, and retiring comfortably by a certain age. These dreams are not selfish, nor is the effort we put into them, including socking money away. Those dreams benefit you, your family, and they benefit the society in which you live. Your dream home provides jobs for the people who will build it and maintain it. Your educated child will be a productive employee or employer, generating ideas to improve the standard of living and quality of life of others. The ability to retire comfortably reduces the burden on fellow taxpayers as you can now provide for your own needs, not becoming dependent on the provincial health care system in particular and the federal government in general.

Also, if we don't practice financial planning we could find ourselves ill-prepared in an emergency. We could be missing out on opportunities to use our assets or resources in as efficient a manner as possible, and we could end up paying more income tax over a longer period of time than was necessary.

I want to warn you that sometimes your planner will tell you things you don't want to hear or give you recommendations you don't want to carry out. Sometimes your planner will depress you! I'm sure that many of my clients have sat there secretly wishing a tornado would touch down and take me away from their kitchen table while leaving the rest of the house intact.

For example, I use a computer program which helps me establish for clients what they need to be putting aside to have their desired standard of living throughout retirement. I ask my clients to think backwards. I ask them to tell me in today's dollars what kind of after-tax retirement income they would like to have; to come up with a round, ballpark figure.

Let's say $50,000 annually, which means they want to have in retirement the kind of life that $50,000 after-tax right now would buy them. They want that "standard of living." Then we look at the following factors:

- ❑ How long we think they are going to live
- ❑ How many years they have until retirement
- ❑ What rate of return their investments could generate
- ❑ What could be the average rate of inflation over time
- ❑ And how much money they've already set aside

The program does the calculation and says in order to support those variables, this is what you need to be investing now, on a monthly basis. I warn clients that the result of this exercise is usually disheartening; that financial planning isn't always fun. It's a lot like standing in front of the mirror naked; perhaps not a pretty sight but it shows us where we could be doing some work.

Remember that financial planning is a snapshot in time, it's not static. Your Certified Financial Planner will provide you with a plan and walk you through it so that you understand its contents and the strategies it outlines. But you will both go back and review it as your personal circumstances, your expectations and the legislative and economic environment in which you are working change. For example, any federal budget that affects how you are taxed or at what level, will send you to the drawing board to re-evaluate your plan and its variables. Sometimes a financial planner is the bearer of bad news and sometimes the remedy isn't very palatable. But ultimately, you've hired that person to tell you what you need to know. And he or she may be telling you something you don't fully understand at first, so you've also hired an educator. Therefore, it is important to choose someone whom you value because there will be communication both ways. Look at your

111

prospective planner and think, could I take good news *and* bad news from this person? Would they have the integrity and diplomacy to tell me what I need to know? Would they treat me with respect?

After you begin working together, your relationship will progress. You may meet with your CFP many times during the year if your financial affairs are complex or your family situation is complicated. Or you may meet less frequently if the plan is working, or your plan is simple and the objectives are being met. When clients and I start working together and we've agreed on a series of strategies, it might take us a full year of meetings before we've implemented all the steps, after which it is a question of maintenance until the client's circumstances change again. Both you, your plan, and your financial planner need to be flexible. But the plan doesn't replace you; your initiative is still the key to making your financial plan work.

> **"Be sure you have realistic expectations of what your advisor can and cannot do. One of the biggest reasons people experience dissatisfaction with their advisor is because they may not clearly understand exactly what their role is. Financial advisors do just that – advise."**
>
> Joanne Thomas Yaccato, *Balancing Act*

I wish you and your financial planner a very long and satisfying relationship.

Chapter Thirteen

The 6 Steps

"Little Piglet – held back by imaginings and fears, yearning to be Someone – is the last animal one might expect to accomplish anything of importance. And yet Piglet is the material from which heroes are made."

Benjamin Hoff, *The Te of Piglet*

There are 6 main steps in the financial planning process. These steps involve common sense and the process itself isn't very different from any other planning you would do.

1. **Identify** what it is you want to achieve – what are your financial desires?

2. **Gather** the information available which could shed light on your current situation and your new goals. This is your reality check. What is the current state of your affairs? What do you need to know?

3. **Analyze** the information you've pulled together to generate ideas about what you want to do differently and how you are going to do it.

4. **Decide** on the actual steps you're going to take: This is where you research your options and develop "the plan."

5. **Implement** the plan – you need to take action and you will start making the changes you've chosen. You have designed these changes to work to your benefit and advantage. These could be small, incremental changes or larger "cold turkey" ones if you've decided that's the way to go.

6. **Monitor** your plan and adjust it where necessary. This is an ongoing exercise. You may be adjusting it because you've achieved one goal and now you are ready to work on the next one. Or you could be adjusting your plan because of changing circumstances i.e. you've been laid-off, you're moving to a new city, you've had a baby, you've inherited money, you're going back to school, etc.

It is your plan. It is your baby. Don't neglect your plan. Go back and review it regularly so you can congratulate yourself on how far you have come. Make changes whenever you need to. Build on the momentum of your past triumphs. Seed, water and grow your plan.

"Every action you take, whether it is directly successful or not, adds additional energy to your path. Because of this, everything you do works towards creating eventual success ...Creating the results you want will get easier and easier."
Robert Fritz, *The Path of Least Resistance*

Chapter Fourteen

Goal Setting

> "Effort without a goal is just that: effort. On the other hand, virtually nothing on earth can stop a person pursuing a goal clearly in sight."
>
> Denis Waitley, *Timing is Everything*

What would I like to accomplish?

Over your lifetime you will have many financial goals. Some will be short term, such as, "By this time next year I'd like to have $ _____ in my cushion account." Others will be long term and you'll spend most of your life working toward them, such as caring for your retirement nest egg. To prevent yourself from being overwhelmed and to make it easier to stay focussed, pick 3 financial goals you would like to work on over the next 6 months to a year. Please know that you will go back often to re-examine these goals, so you don't have to get it perfect you just have to get it started.

On the next page I have listed some possible goals, which may jog your thinking, but first I'd like you to go and grab your daytimer, calendar, agenda or palm pilot. Circle today, the day you established your financial goals, now mark-off the day(s) you will review them.

If you have a lot of changes you'd like to make, or mini-goals you would like to achieve, you may decide to meet with yourself more often, i.e. set aside one hour every other Sunday afternoon to review your progress. Or you may choose a semi-annual schedule such as spring and fall (when you change your clocks and check the batteries in your smoke detectors) or a winter/summer schedule around January 1st (New Year's Day) and July 1st (Canada Day). If you replace your toothbrush regularly you can use that schedule too. Set up a timeframe which works for you. There is no point going further unless you make a date with yourself to review and carry on the good work you are starting. This is a gift – the very best birthday gift you can give yourself. In fact, since you should review all your hard work at least once a year, do it around your birthday and give yourself a colourful bouquet of flowers – it will be a very rewarding date.

Possible financial goals in no particular order:

- ❑ Pay down (pay off) student debt
- ❑ Pay down (eliminate) credit card debt
- ❑ Start an account to save for the downpayment on a home
- ❑ Start a regular contribution plan to my retirement savings/investment account
- ❑ Contribute to an education fund/account for my children, grandchildren or myself
- ❑ Ask my friends for referrals to good estate lawyers and/or tax preparers or accountants
- ❑ Start learning about (or learn more about) estate planning
- ❑ Learn about the different kinds of life insurance
- ❑ Decide who should be my executor(s) and who should hold power of attorney
- ❑ Decide who should be the guardian(s) of my children
- ❑ Get my will updated or completed (including my powers of attorney)

- Look into funeral options and pre-payment plans
- Get a better handle on how my income is taxed
- Get my taxes done
- Start learning about how I can save taxes
- Write down every penny I spend over the next month – every penny!
- Reduce the number of fast food/restaurant meals I eat
- Start asking my friends what is their best financial planning advice
- Establish my net worth and decide how much I want to increase it each year
- Review my benefits plan at work and ask questions if I don't understand my coverage
- Look into re-negotiating my mortgage, could this be an option for me?
- Better understand the flexibility of my mortgage – could I make lump sum payments?
- Look into furthering my education as an investment – what would I need to do to make more money?
- Look at the pros & cons of a potential career change down the road
- Review my job prospects for five years from now
- Review my company's prospects for five years from now
- Reduce the number of credit cards I own
- Start a filing system for all the statements which come into my home
- Look into ways to reduce the cost of car insurance
- Look into ways to reduce the use of my car
- Start saving to buy (or lease) a new or used car
- Look into the differences between buying or leasing a car
- Review my family situation to establish if my parents might become financially dependent on me
- Increase my retirement savings contributions by a certain percentage each year
- Start saving for my retirement outside of my RRSP
- Look into the cost of retirement homes

- ❏ Look into the cost of nursing homes
- ❏ Research Long Term Care insurance
- ❏ Research Critical Illness insurance
- ❏ Save for a vacation
- ❏ Save for a wedding
- ❏ Save for new furniture
- ❏ Save for renovations
- ❏ Other goals:

> **"Our only excuse is ignorance. We are unaware of our capabilities. We do not realize that each of us is the marvel of the universe."**
> George Sheehan, M.D., *Personal Best*

OK, now you're ready: Over the next 6 months to a year I will be working on the following 3 financial goals:

Today's date: _____

1. _____

2. _____

3. _____

Notes:_____

Notes:_____

Notes:_____

I will be reviewing these 3 goals on the following dates:

1st Review: _____

2nd Review: _____

3rd Review: _____

4th Review: _____

Chapter Fifteen

Who am I?

> "If one woman has done it, so can you – and if not, why not you? … There's no reason you can't be the first. Someone has to be."
>
> Sarah Ban Breathnach, *Simple Abundance*

Putting Myself Down on Paper

Have you ever put yourself down on paper? Unlike standing in front of the mirror naked, this can be an enjoyable activity. It's interesting and amusing in a detached kind of way. This isn't your résumé or your CV. You're not trying to convince anybody. You're not trying to prove anything. It's not a question of worthiness but of fact. Of all the times and places you could have been alive, you are here right now. You weren't born a peasant in the middle ages. You aren't working in a factory at the end of the 19th century. You are alive in the 21st century and these are the current facts about you.

While this is actually dry stuff, and ultimately is of assistance to those who will manage your affairs if you become incapacitated or when you die, you will also find it helpful because this gathering of information about you is another snapshot in time. It is not a beautiful photograph. It doesn't mirror your being or reflect your soul. This is you, black and white on paper. It is an inventory of information – that's all. But being able to look at yourself in a detached manner is reassuring – you exist; other people are affected by you and you affect other people. You will realize you are an essential piece of the puzzle because you are a part of what makes the world go round at this very minute. In other words, your existence on paper, in black and white, will show that you are not an island. You are part of the current geography. Everybody counts.

This is an exercise in organization, and it is worth it. This information should be filed with your important documents in a safe and secure place, where you can get at it, and where those who would pick up the pieces if something happened to you, can also find it. This information will be of value to your powers of attorney and to your executors – we will be discussing their roles in a later chapter.

Because it is formatted in a dry, factual manner some people will find it easier than others to use as a springboard to making changes. We are each inspired differently. If you would like to live somewhere else, if your home is not really a "home" or not where you want to be, the data below might help to crystalize your vision. Some of us see a picture or advertisement and we keep that in our mind's eye as the beacon. Ah, that's what our dream home will look like one day. Do you remember the movie "The Good-bye Girl" with Marsha Mason and Richard Dreyfus? Marsha's character had a picture of a beautifully decorated room from a magazine, which she then had recreated down to every detail. (And do you remember she broke into tears when the room was completed?) For some, our dream is visual and an image on paper or in our mind is what inspires us.

Others of us will look at our address and decide in 5 years time I'm going to live in a different city, in a particular part of town, I'm going to own not rent. Instead of updating my inventory with information about my landlord and my lease, it will be changed to show my new address and a mortgage. In other words some of us dream in colour and some of us dream in black and white. For some our dreams are fuelled by imagination, for others our dreams are enlightened by data. That's okay, if you want to make changes - the inspiration can come in any form. If you find this inventory inspires you to make changes which lead to greater financial security, then the exercise was well worth it.

You may complete the inventory below and be quite satisfied: you might like what you see on paper because it shows how far you have come. You can remember when the only things you had in your name were hand-me-down furniture and milk crates of used textbooks. An inventory of information about you would have drawn a lot of blanks back in those days.

As a result of this exercise you may realize there are too many blanks now. If you died tonight your next of kin wouldn't know where to begin to get everything taken care of because even you don't know pertinent information about yourself. What if before we could play in paradise we had to come back as ghosts and tidy up our own messes? How long would you be here looking for missing documents, insurance policies and tax information, dealing with unsympathetic customer service personnel, making your way through bureaucracy and red-tape, perhaps paying extended legal fees because you didn't have your ducks in a row? Remember when you weren't allowed to go outside and play until your room was clean and your homework done? It's the same thing on a cosmic level. When the sun is shining and the birds are singing, make sure you're ready to be outside playing without guilt and without regrets. Enjoy paradise knowing you've done your homework, and you haven't left a mess behind for someone else to figure out and to clean up, no matter how long it may take them.

The basis of an inventory is below. Feel free to make copies, but you may also want to set this up on your own computer. You can use a simple word processing or spreadsheet program and adapt it for your personal data. (If you have 6 siblings, 5 children, 12 grandchildren and 3 great-grandchildren, you will find there is not enough space in our example.) Please make sure this information is **stored safely**, the last thing you want is to have your identity stolen. However, I also suggest that you have a second copy in case a diskette or paper copy is destroyed.

First, read through the inventory and complete it with the information you already know, that is information you know by heart, or numbers which are easy to look up. Then go back and decide which blank spots you are going to work on next. You probably won't be able to complete this in one sitting; there will be documents you have to find, phone calls you need to make and even appointments to sit down with your advisors to review your coverage or holdings.

When you feel you have written enough information for this document to be helpful then inform your executors and powers of attorney of its existence and where it is kept. It would be a shame for you to put in all this work only to have your executor re-invent the wheel (which would be even more time consuming than completing the exercise in the first place) because he or she didn't know you had done the preparation. You will update your inventory as your circumstances change and they usually do from year to year. You won't want to have a number of copies out there which you can potentially lose track of. But the one or two people who you would rely on in an emergency should know where they can access this consolidated data. As a Certified Financial Planner, if a client asked me to keep a copy of their personal inventory in their file I would do so. This is very confidential information and you need to entrust it to people who are caring and conscientious.

If you already suspect completing this inventory is going to be a challenge – something you will have to force yourself to do, then attach a date and reward to its completion. I am a firm believer in self-bribery. In fact, feel free to reward yourself at various stages of its completion. You can use this strategy for other activities in this book. The reward doesn't have to be monetary, but it does have to be self-indulgent and self-congratulatory.

Please fill-in these blanks:

I will have my self-inventory completed by:

_____ (date)

My reward for completing it by:

_____ (repeat the date)

will be:

_____

Attached to your inventory should be your Net Worth Statement which we will complete in the next chapter. A Net Worth Statement lists everything you own and it's value as well as everything you owe (to whom and how much). But a

Net Worth Statement does not tell you where the documentation can be found for what you own (the papers for your house for example) and what you owe (your latest mortgage statement). The inventory below provides room for this kind of information and if it is not enough space, please include other sheets of paper making sure to keep all your gathered data **safely** together.

A Personal Inventory of Information

For: _____

Dated: _____

Full name:

_____

Address:

_____

Date of birth: _____

Next of kin:

Name (relationship)	Address & Phone/e-mail
_____	_____
_____	_____
_____	_____
_____	_____

_____   _____

_____   _____

_____   _____

_____   _____

My Power of Attorneys and Will were last revised (when):

_____

Copies of these documents are (where):

_____

My Power of Attorney(s) for Health Care decisions:

Name   Address & Phone/e-mail

_____   _____

_____   _____

My Power of Attorney(s) for Property decisions:

Name   Address & Phone/e-mail

_____   _____

_____   _____

My Executor(s):

Name   Address & Phone/e-mail

_____   _____

_____   _____

My Lawyer(s):

Name   Address & Phone/e-mail

_____   _____

_____   _____

My Financial Advisor(s):

Name   Address & Phone/e-mail

_____   _____

_____   _____

My Insurance Agents(s):

Name   Address & Phone/e-mail

_____   _____

_____   _____

My Accountant/Tax Preparer:

Name   Address & Phone/e-mail

_____   _____

Forms of identification:

                              Number
Birth Certificate: _____
Where it is kept: _____

                              Number
Social Insurance: _____
Where it is kept: _____

                              Number
Passport: _____
Where it is kept: _____

                              Number
Health Card: _____
Where it is kept: _____

                              Number
Organ Donation Card: _____
Where it is kept: _____

Other Identification:
                              Number
_____: _____
Where it is kept: _____

Other Identification:

Number

_____:

Where it is kept: _____

                                    _____

Other Identification:

Number

_____:

Where it is kept: _____

                                    _____

Current Employer:

Co. Name   Contact phone/e-mail

_____   _____

Pension &/or Insurance Benefits with an employer
(or previous employers):

Type of benefit:

_____

Co. Name   Contact phone/e-mail

_____   _____

Type of benefit:

_____

Co. Name   Contact phone/e-mail

_____   _____

Type of benefit:

_____

Co. Name   Contact phone/e-mail

_____   _____

Personally owned Insurance Policies:

Type of Insurance:

_____

Co. Name   Contact phone/e-mail

_____   _____

Type of Insurance:

_____

Co. Name   Contact phone/e-mail

_____   _____

Type of Insurance:

_____

Co. Name   Contact phone/e-mail

_____   _____

Type of Insurance:

_____

Co. Name   Contact phone/e-mail

_____   _____

Documentation:

A listing of different documents & where they are kept. Documents pertaining to:

House:

_____

Investment Property:

_____

Mortgage(s):

_____

Mortgage(s):

_____

Apartment:

_____

Cottage:

_____

Car:

_____

Car:

_____

Bank Accounts:

_____

Savings Bonds:

_____

Retirement Plans:

_____

Investment Accounts:

_____

Education Plans:

_____

Utilities:

_____

_____

_____

Credit Cards:

_____

_____

_____

Tax returns:

_____

_____

Charities:

_____

_____

_____

Funeral Arrangements:

_____

_____

Inherited Documents:

_____

_____

(ie. Grandparents' marriage certificate, birth certificates, family heirlooms)

Money/Items
Owed *by* me:

_____

_____

Money/Items
Owed *by* me:

_____

_____

Money/Items
Owed to me:

_____

_____

Money/Items
Owed to me:

_____

_____

Notes:

_____

_____

_____

_____

_____

_____

> "Actually *everything* is always evolving, and
> interestingly, evolution is not toward more complexity
> as we might suspect but toward simplicity."
>
> Sue Patton Thoele, *The Woman's Book of Soul*

Chapter Sixteen

Where am I now?

"Many people live as if life were a dress rehearsal for some later date. It isn't."

Richard Carlson, *Don't Sweat the Small Stuff*

There are two components to this activity. The first is to figure out your net worth. This means writing down all the things you own and their approximate value, then listing all the amounts you owe, to whom and how much. You want to add up what you own and subtract what you owe, in order to come up with a single figure. This is very important. You need to attach a dollar figure to your name.

Having said that, please know there can be no monetary value attached to you as a person. There is only one you, and you are *priceless*. You are here to make the world a better place. What you offer is unique and you are needed. "No less than the trees and the stars, you have a right to be here ..." But to ensure that you have looked after yourself, and that you have put yourself in a position to fulfill your special role, you need to be financially aware and self-sufficient.

Your Net Worth Statement is a tool of measurement. It can tell you if you need to spend more time building your assets or not, and most of us do. Your net worth does not measure your worth as a person. It measures your financial worth, which is an indication of how secure or confident you can be about your circumstances, within our current market economy, while looking toward your future needs.

Your net worth is a straightforward equation. We are not going to make it any more complicated than it needs to be. What is important is that we actually generate it. Once we have produced our Net Worth Statement, we only have to update it later on. Mine is a simple computer spreadsheet, which I revise quarterly. I'm the type of person who gets excited when my investment statements arrive in the mail and it's time to look at my personal tally. Of course, because I'm invested in the markets through some stocks and a number of mutual funds, my net worth doesn't always go up each quarter. It fluctuates. Sometimes it goes down for a few quarters in a row. It's sort of like my weight – it will go up again! I'm experienced enough to know that any weight loss (and negative investment return) is usually temporary.

And I honestly get a kick out of putting a dollar figure to my name, because it feels like a game. It's real but it's not real. It's real in the sense that in order to live, function and be productive in this world I need to value my net worth and I enjoy being good at the skills which allow me to track and build my financial security. It's not real in the sense that if I am accountable when I die, that's not what I will be judged upon. I remember driving past a graveyard in New Jersey about 15 years ago and seeing little American flags stuck in the ground beside the tombstones. This wasn't a military site, and it struck me as odd to see graves marked by a country's flag. Maybe it's my strange Canadian perspective, but I thought surely once you die your nationality doesn't matter. Aren't we all citizens? Aren't we all stewards of our planet? Children of the universe? At death I don't believe our nationality will matter any more than our net worth. What will matter is how we lived. But while we are here, our Net Worth Statement helps us to be accountable and to be responsible for ourselves. There is a difference between the quality of our life and our standard of living. We want to work on both; we want to make time for both.

Below is a template you can use to establish your net worth. You can copy this or re-create it elsewhere, just make sure you keep it straightforward.

Net Worth Statement for:

_____

Date last revised:

_____

Assets:

Market Value of:

House   + $ _____

Cottage   + $ _____

Property   + $ _____

Real Estate + $ _____

Registered Retirement Plans:

     Cash/Savings   + $_____

     Bonds   + $_____

     Mutual Funds   + $_____

     Stocks   + $_____

     Other _____   + $_____

     Other _____   + $_____

Non-Registered Investments:

     Cash / Savings   + $_____

     Bonds   + $_____

     Mutual Funds   + $_____

     Stocks   + $_____

     Other _____   + $_____

     Other _____   + $_____

Liabilities:

Mortgage   < - $_____>

Owed to: _____

     Interest rate: _____   Expiry date: _____

Mortgage   < - $ _____ >

Owed to: _____

     Interest rate: _____   Expiry date: _____

Line of Credit   < - $ _____ >

Owed to: _____

     Interest rate: _____   Expiry date: _____

Car Loan/Lease   < - $ _____ >

Owed to: _____

     Interest rate: _____   Expiry date: _____

Student Loan   < - $_____ >

Owed to: _____

     Interest rate: _____   Expiry date: _____

Student Loan   < - $_____ >

Owed to: _____

     Interest rate: _____   Expiry date: _____

Credit Card   < - $ _____ >

Owed to: _____

     Interest rate: _____   Expiry date: _____

Credit Card   < - $ _____ >

Owed to: _____

     Interest rate: _____   Expiry date: _____

Personal Loan   < - $_____ >

Owed to: _____

     Interest rate: _____   Expiry date: _____

Taxes Owing   < - $_____ >

Owed to: _____

     Interest rate: _____   Expiry date: _____

Other $ Owing   < - $_____ >

Owed to: _____

     Interest rate: _____   Expiry date: _____

Net Worth: $ _____

(Total of all the "+" and all the "< - >")

Please note that your Net Worth Statement does not include the value of your vehicles (a diminishing asset at best), your furnishings, artwork, heirlooms or personal items. We've tried to keep this Statement as simple as possible, and we are working with ballpark figures to some degree. The importance of this activity is to get one bottom-line figure and then to watch that figure grow as you regularly update the information this Statement captures. You may update your Net Worth Statement quarterly, but your goal is to see an annual increase. In some years that increase may be attributed to your real estate holdings, in other years the markets will have gone up, increasing the value of your mutual funds. Or your overall net worth may increase because you have made a concentrated effort to pay down debt. Your Net Worth Statement will fluctuate but you want to see an upward trend over time.

Some people feel they should include in their Net Worth Statement the value of money or assets they think they will inherit one day. Don't ever count your chickens until the eggs have hatched. You either own an asset or you don't. If an asset it is not legally in your possession right now, you don't own it and it shouldn't be included.

When it comes to debt, first try to pay down the debt you are carrying which is charging the highest interest rate. That may mean reading the fine print on your statements, but again it is worth the effort to know this information. By completing the Net Worth Statement your debt-reducing strategies will jump out at you – you'll know where your resources need to go – which debt needs to be paid first and fastest. With respect to your mortgage, I suggest to clients that they top-up their registered retirement savings plans (RRSPs) and then take the refund and put it toward the mortgage. The majority of the time, the percentage you will save in taxes will be much greater than your mortgage's interest rate. And once you've paid income tax to the government rarely can you get any of it back. If interest rates have dropped considerably since you originally signed your mortgage papers, it might make sense to renegotiate your mortgage and/or look at switching from a monthly payment plan to a semi-monthly or bi-weekly schedule. Nine times out of ten, it makes sense to maximize your retirement savings first and then apply what you've saved in taxes to your mortgage. At the end of the day, you want more and more assets building in your name including your RRSPs – that's what gives you greater control and greater flexibility. ("Freedom … Just imagine.")

When I do this exercise with clients, they are usually surprised by the resulting Net Worth figure. Sometimes they didn't know they were worth that much, other times they are upset to see how little they are worth on paper. Again I reassure them that it doesn't measure their value as a human being. And if that doesn't help, I remind them that like most of us, if they have insurance, they are probably worth a lot more dead than alive! I try to provide what comic relief I can. There is always something you can do. And it is never too late to start. If we meet again in six months and my client sees a change – a positive difference – that is proof and incentive to keep working at the plan.

"Goals are there to help you and support you in your true purpose. Goals can be made in the spirit that life is an enjoyable game to be played, and one that can be deeply rewarding."

Shakti Gawain, *Creative Visualization*

What's measured gets attention. Just by tracking your net worth regularly, while reviewing your goals and deciding on the strategies or changes you would like to make, you will see your "bottom line" figure increase over time because it will be important to you. And it is important.

The second component to looking at where you are now, is to establish how much money you bring into your home, assess where it goes, and then decide how much you will allocate to your goals. What resources, both time and money, are you willing to put toward making your dreams come true? How do you eat an elephant? One bite at a time. Always remember that it should be empowering to pursue your goals. Your financial health and longevity are worth fighting for. When a challenge is empowering it inspires one to act and its results are intrinsically rewarding. You will be glad you rose to the challenge.

Earlier, I suggested the following equation: Financial Planning = Stress Relief. One of the very best ways to reduce your stress level every day, day in and day out, is to live beneath your means. It makes sense that the higher your income the easier this would be, but you also need to be very aware of what it costs for you to live. You want to decide what is important and you want to know where your money goes. I do not subscribe to the idea that we get to have it all, nor do we get to do it all. I believe we are called upon to make choices. We are called upon to make good choices. Choices which are right for us and the people who depend on us, choices which are considerate of the earth which sustains us and the others who live on it. In order to have more financial security and less environmental damage we should be looking for ways to live beneath our means. And this type of lifestyle can be a source of amusement as well as satisfaction. I love getting compliments on clothes that are 10 to 20 years old. I take pride in my little Toyota when it's parked beside a massive vehicle at a red light. The Scottish frugality I learned from Grandma Duncan has worked to my benefit.

I'm not a big believer in budgets unless designing and following budgets makes you happy, in which case, go for it. If you enjoy sticking to a budget, then you know the whole purpose of doing so, your motivation, is to have more money in your pocket at the end of the week. And therefore more money in your bank account at the end of the month to apply to your lifetime goals.

If budgeting does not sound like fun to you, that's okay. You may be interested in a Money Map. Rather than looking forward and setting up a budget which feels punitive, why not look back and see where you can more easily make changes. A budget can feel punishing and oppressive, but a Money Map implies that you are smart, discerning and flexible. Completing a Money Map means reviewing or "mapping out" where you've spent money in the recent past and deciding for your own satisfaction how you could spend it differently in the future. A sample, blank Money Map follows at the end of this chapter. Feel free to take a look at it now and to make copies, or to revise it. This can be a very useful tool; it's a checklist and a starting point. And sometimes it's an eye-opener. It does not take long to complete. It doesn't need to be correct to the penny. But it does need to be reflective of **your** expenses, so it is worth taking the time to calculate your answers.

Basically, there are three columns:

The first is a list of possible places you spend money on a regular basis. "Regular basis" means everything from daily purchases i.e. A cup of coffee on your way to work, to annual expenses such as the renewal of your diver's license.

The second column asks how much you spend on these items on a monthly basis, and the third column asks you to come up with an annual figure. It's a good idea to complete columns two and three even if there is some pro-rating involved. For example, when you ask yourself "where does all the money go?" you need to consider what you spend on gift-giving each year: Birthdays, Valentine's weddings, Christmas, Mother's/Father's Day, anniversaries, graduations etc., even memorial donations. It might be easier to mentally add up what you probably spend on all those occasions throughout the year. Write this figure in the annual column and then divide it by 12 and write the equivalent figure in the monthly column. You would likely do the same for vacation spending; come up with an average annual amount then divide it by 12 to get your monthly spending.

Whereas for your cable, cell phone or hairdressing costs, you may not have thought about these on an annual basis. It would be pretty easy to figure out the average monthly cost of your cell phone if you've kept the past few bills. Take this figure and multiply it by 12 for the annual cost. You might be surprised by the annual cost of your hair – suddenly what colour it is doesn't seem to be as important any more. If you discover that you are spending more on your hair than you are putting into your retirement savings each year, you'll be very glad you finished this exercise. Better late than never.

After you have completed the Money Map, you will want to establish a bottom line figure of what it costs for you to live in your current lifestyle on a monthly and annual basis. That is only half the fun. The second half of the exercise is to pull out copies of your pay stubs and/or your past income tax returns – pull as many as you can find. We need to compare your cost of living to your take-home pay.

"Did you know we'll spend more time planning a wedding and a honeymoon than we ever will on our personal finances?"

Linda Leatherdale, *Money is a Girl's Best Friend*

Once you have finished your Money Map, please complete the following statement:

My take-home pay for last year was: $ _____

(If you can't find pay stubs or the tax slips your employer(s) issued, then go back and look at your bank statement or bank book. Again, it might take a bit of detective work, but you can calculate your annual take-home pay. It's not a mystery. You've come this far in the book. Just remember the little train engine who kept repeating to himself: "I think I can, I think I can, I think I can ...")

My annual living expenses were: $ _____
(data from my Money Map)

The amount of money I currently am able to put toward my **3 financial goals** *is:*

$ _____
(take-home pay minus living expenses)

Now, what do you think about that figure? Even if it is far smaller than you would like it to be, it's yours and you should be proud of the work you did to identify your uncommitted income. Give yourself a big round of applause. Yes, that means clapping out loud.

Well you've decided on some of the financial goals you wish to pursue and you've taken a very thorough look at your current situation. As a result, you may have drawn a few conclusions. Two thoughts are probably coming to mind: how can I best allocate uncommitted income to my three main goals? And how can I increase that uncommitted income? After all, financial planning means looking out for your financial health and ensuring that your money lasts at least as long as you do.

One of the areas you may have chosen to focus on was debt reduction, in which case know how much debt you have and where it is (who you owe), and you've looked at the interest rate you are paying on each loan. The next step is to prioritize your debt repayment. Who is going to get how much and when? The key factor will be the interest rate. The higher the interest rate the sooner you will want to pay off that debt. Most debt which individuals carry is not tax deductible, which has been our assumption here. (If you've decided you want to explore the differences between deductible and non-deductible debt as an investment strategy, you will want to meet with a CFP.)

Having completed your Money Map, and perhaps a few revised versions of it, you've established a monthly figure to allocate toward your goals, which is the difference between your take-home pay and your living costs. This is **your** figure, regardless of whether it's $50 or $5,000 - the important thing is that you have discovered where your resources are and you have taken charge of where you are going to spend them in the future.

A word of caution, while common sense, let alone higher mathematics, might suggest you put all your "goal money" towards paying down debt before you put any toward savings, this can feel defeating. If you have consumer debt with high interest rates, i.e. charge cards, credit cards, loans or lines of credit, I definitely recommend putting all your resources towards those debts. However, if you have a mortgage (or a line of credit) with low or reasonable interest rates, focus on making tax-deductible contributions to your retirement savings plan then take the refund those contributions generate and apply that to debt. You can work on two goals at the same time. You don't have to wait until you are completely debt-free to build up your savings, whether it's a cushion, an emergency fund or a retirement plan. If you are committed to being better off financially there is no reason you can't accomplish both objectives. Paying down debt is the right thing to do, but it's not a fun thing to do. Putting money into your RRSP is the right thing to do, and it's a fun thing to do. So why not do both?

When it comes to mortgages, I've seen people who have been obsessed at paying them off. They have stepped-up their payment schedule so much that the stress of making the new higher payments seems to outweigh the satisfaction of a shorter mortgage. You want to maintain balance and flexibility in all your financial plans, including paying down debt.

The following is a tip regarding debt owed on credit cards: even if you can't afford to increase the amount you are paying monthly, you can break-up the payment during the month. Let's say you are putting an extra $300 a month on a credit card to eliminate the balance owing. Instead of paying $300 only at month's end, break-up the payment and put $150 on the credit card at mid-month with the remaining $150 going on the card at the end of the month. This strategy will ultimately leave you with more money in your pocket because the interest is accruing daily. Even if you have an extra $20 in your wallet at the end of the week, walk into the bank and plunk it down on the card. Every day you have an outstanding balance that debt becomes more expensive to carry. The sooner you pay down credit card debt, the less that debt will cost you and the sooner your money will be your own.

Sometimes I may be called in to meet with a prospective client because this person feels trapped. Let's call her "Julie." Julie doesn't know how she can escape from living paycheque to paycheque. We review Julie's current financial situation and I suggest that she needs to start putting $100 a month in an RRSP. "Oh Heather, I don't have $100 at the end of the month." But I know this is what Julie really wants to do. "Okay, can you save two twoonies a day?" Julie thinks about this and usually the answer is "yes." If Julie cut out buying a fancy coffee in the morning with a mega-muffin, or maybe she doesn't really need a chocolate bar most afternoons, and if she's been buying lottery tickets for four years but she's never won more than $10, then Julie usually decides she can save two twoonies a day. That's great I tell her. Now she's happily committed herself, because a monthly $100 RRSP contribution is less than two twoonies per weekday – she can still spend them on the weekend! Since the refund she gets from the government can be applied against her debt, she's chosen to build a nest egg, get a tax break and pay down debt all at the same time.

Congratulations, to Julie she's on her way.

Money Map

	$ Monthly	*$ Annually*
Regular Savings	_____	_____
Payments on Loans	_____	_____
Payments on Lines of Credit	_____	_____
Payments on Car Leases	_____	_____
Payments on Credit Cards	_____	_____
Mortgage (principal, int. & taxes)	_____	_____
Groceries (including: cleaning supplies, bulk items, pet food, bottled water, toiletries, etc.)	_____	_____
Shelter - Rent	_____	_____
Repairs	_____	_____
Insurance	_____	_____
Utilities	_____	_____
Phone & Cable (plus cell & internet)	_____	_____
Transportation - Gas	_____	_____
Maintenance	_____	_____
Insurance	_____	_____
License Renewal	_____	_____
Parking / Cab fares	_____	_____
Public transportation	_____	_____
Life / Disability Ins. premiums	_____	_____
Medical / Dental premiums & / or expenses	_____	_____
Clothing	_____	_____
Other		
1) _____	_____	_____
2) _____	_____	_____
3) _____	_____	_____
4) _____	_____	_____
5) _____	_____	_____
Sub-totals	_____	_____

152

Time Period: _____

	$ Monthly	*$ Annually*
Child care expenses	_____	_____
Child support / Alimony	_____	_____
Elder care expenses	_____	_____
Your Education (courses, books, fees)	_____	_____
Your Child's Education (courses, books, fees)	_____	_____
Recreation:		
Meals out / friends in	_____	_____
Beer / Wine	_____	_____
Sports / Hobbies / Clubs	_____	_____
Subscriptions	_____	_____
CDs / Videos	_____	_____
Books / Movies	_____	_____
Computer expenses	_____	_____
Gifts:		
Charitable Donations	_____	_____
Holiday gifts / spending	_____	_____
Birthday / Wedding gifts	_____	_____
Vacations / Holidays	_____	_____
Services:		
Dry cleaning	_____	_____
Lawn care / Snow removal	_____	_____
Cleaning service	_____	_____
Personal Trainer	_____	_____
Vet / pet expenses	_____	_____
Massages / Manicures	_____	_____
Hair appointments	_____	_____
_____	_____	_____
Sub-totals	_____	_____
TOTAL	_____	_____

Chapter Seventeen

Orpha T.

Orpha is 75 years old. She never married nor had children. She is a retired nurse.

What studies did Canada offer you as a nurse that you wanted to pursue?

A degree. I didn't have any family here when I came to Hamilton, Ontario and started at McMaster University. I was on my own.

Do you have any regrets having left the Caribbean?

I have no regrets whatsoever. I was always treated fairly. If you respect people, they respect you. I think maybe I came with the right attitude. The things that I wouldn't do in Barbados, I wouldn't do here. Even though I would be "one in the desert." You know, I was pretty definite about ideas and I've always been like that.

If a person has integrity, it doesn't matter geographically where they are. There are certain ways you will act and behave and other ways you won't.

Integrity is so important. I knew a few nurses who lived in Toronto, but in Hamilton I didn't know anyone there and I was adopted by the Canadians.

Your mom said she didn't think you were ever going to get married because you turned down some pretty good offers in Barbados. Did you think that you would go back?

Yes, I thought that after a few years I would go back and share my knowledge, but it never seemed to work out that way. I was working as a theatre [operating room] nurse when I left. When you come into a new country, it's nice to see how some of the other people in that country live. After I did my Bachelor's at McMaster, I moved on to Ottawa.

How long have you been in Ottawa?

Oh goodness gracious, it's been so long I've forgotten. I came to Canada in 1956. I think it was in 1959 I began working at the Civic Hospital. Then I wanted to do geriatric nursing and I worked at a Catholic, geriatric hospital from 1960 to 1963, St. Vincent's. Then I went back to the Civic, which became home for me. I've worked with many, many nurses over the years.

When we were talking on the phone, you offered what I thought was a great line: "The first day you start working should be the first day you start saving for your retirement."

I have said that to a number of nurses over the years, and especially the younger ones, those are the ones I would always straighten out. The ones who never think about it, who said, "What are you talking about?"

I think it's true, it's absolutely true. I always say that a young age is a wonderful thing if you have the knowledge. But it doesn't work that way. You become so much more knowledgeable over the years than you were in your twenties. You think you know everything at that age. They'd

156

say, "What are you talking about? Saving, what's that? The faster I work for it, the faster I could spend it."

And you were no different in your twenties?

No. Are you kidding?

Orpha, when did you start taking responsibility financially for yourself and looking toward the future?

When I moved to Canada my mother was the one who told me it was about time. I'm telling you, that woman ... I must have been in my forties and I remember saying to her, "If you had had a really good education, you could have been the Prime Minister." She always seemed to have a vision for the future. She would tell you some things and by George, you would listen to her. One of her favourite expressions was "Education is not common sense you know." And it is true! Some people have all kinds of education and they are so stupid. And the only thing my mother had was a basic elementary education. But she could read. Anything that was written on paper she would read. The week she died, she insisted on having her daily paper. She said, "I have to know what's going on in the world." Right, mother.

She always said to my father, and I thought this was frank, but he was very understanding and I guess he would take her with a grain of salt, she would say: "You know, you're very good at working for money but you have no common sense for spending it. So I'll spend it for you."

I find that with couples I work with. Sometimes there is a division of labor when it comes to money. They recognize that one of them is better at handling it than the other.

That is true. Fortunately for my brother, sister and I, my father recognized that she really had a good head for figures. I suppose he thought, well she's good at it, let her do it.

So on a trip home your mom said to you "Orpha…"

As a matter of fact, no, she wrote to me. She wrote me and said, "You work for your money. Do you think of spending it all or do you ever think of your future? What will you do when you retire?" She said, "I know that you are very independent and you don't want any person to be taking care of you so it's time to take care of yourself."

Some people, if they'd been in a similar situation where they would get a pension from their employer, wouldn't have been as conscientious as you have been in developing outside savings.

With a mother like mine you just had to be, because she would be after you: "Have you done anything about what I told you?" Oh dear, "Yes mother." I used to call her Lady T. The lady has spoken, we'd better listen. She was a lovely person. She was a strict mother though. I had a lot of respect for her.

Did you inherit a little bit of her personality, because you told me that when you talked to younger nurses they would look at you as though you had two heads?

It's true. But so many of them over the years have done what I suggested. There was another thing I would say to people. When you talk to people about saving, they'll say, "Well I don't have any money to save every month." I would say start small. People have this twisted idea that you have to have "x" hundreds of dollars every month to save for the future. I'd say start small and as you're able to, you add to it. If you can start with $30, start with $30. When you can make it $50 or $100, go right ahead. I was instrumental in getting others to see that view. And I know, because that's exactly what I did.

One aspect of your attitude is that you didn't assume someone else was going to look after you somewhere along the line.

No, are you kidding? No way. If it happens, so be it, but I'm not waiting for that.

Now, you've turned 75. And you are in a situation financially that many women wish they were in at 75. You've done a lot of things right. Tell me about some of those things.

I created a sense of independence and it all stems from that. I could say my upbringing was a factor because, as I said, my mother was strict. But I still remember the week I was leaving for Canada. A very good friend of mother's was over and they were discussing me. This lady said to my mother "Why are you allowing Orpha to go to Canada all alone?" And do you know what my mother said to her? "Why do I stand in the way of my daughter going to Canada? Why would I stand in her way?" Then she said Canada was not that far away. "They have phones there." It was so typical of her. You know for all of the years since I left for Canada, as long as she was alive, every month I sent her a cheque.

So you not only looked after yourself but you helped your mom financially?

Yes, and whether she wanted it or not, that wasn't my business. I sent money for her to do what she wanted to do with it. I mean it wasn't a lot of money. When I first came to

Canada I think I was making $50 a week. But that was $200 a month which was more than I was making at home, even as a ward assistant. So every month I sent her a cheque. And many times I'd go home and realize that the cheque I had sent her was put in the bank for me. She had an account for me. If she didn't need it she'd put it in the bank.

When did you buy your condominium?

I think it was in 1976.

Was that a pretty big decision for you at the time?

Not really. You know, you get tired of paying rent and I thought that was silly. Why pay rent if I am able to get a down payment on an apartment. Instead of paying a rent, I paid a mortgage. I like space. I like my space. I had a friend in yesterday and I said you come and clean out some of these cupboards for me and get rid of the clothes.

It's amazing how much stuff we acquire, isn't it?

I know, tell me about it! Ugh. I will go to the store; they know me so well, the salesclerks tell me about the new things that are in. I tell them that I don't need anything. They say you can still come in and look. That's my downfall. Window shopping is a weak spot, but I am better now because it used to be shoes, shoes to match the outfit.

But there is one thing I have to add, which I think is very positive and that is I hate debt. I have credit cards and I will use them but I don't pay interest – I pay them in 30 days. Another thing I have said to some people, who I thought should have as much common sense as I thought I had, "When you retire make sure you've paid for the apartment you're in. Don't carry a mortgage after retirement. Pay now." I've said, "If you are in the habit of taking a trip every year, forget it for a few years, to pay it down." That's what I did. When I was able to say to myself, "I'm not travelling this year, I'm not travelling next year, and I'm not buying clothes," that was really something for me. I paid it off.

I think that is an important message and I like how strongly you put it, "I hate debt."

I know that if I were to pass on tonight, I think maybe I would owe seven or eight dollars. But that's me. Why would you go and put yourself in debt and not be able to finance your debt? I don't have the level of income I had when I was working anymore. I retired in 1989 at 62.

Do you think you are going to live a long time?

It's hard to know because my mother lived until she was 80. My father died at 66, through an accident as a matter of fact. He retired at 65. He got out of his car and was crossing the street, and out of nowhere a truck hit him. His life was shortened unfortunately. He didn't die on the spot, but he died a few months later. He'd rallied for awhile. And you know it didn't seem fair because he was emergency personnel during the war and his ship was targeted three times and he survived that. He was picked up twice in lifeboats. And he always used to say he wouldn't die at sea. And it was true, he certainly didn't. He had some brothers who lived quite a long time.

My sister who was nine years older than me recently died, while I was over there. I got a call in December to say that she had had a stroke and I should come home to see her. I went to Barbados and she got much better. But then she had a second and a third stroke. The day she had the third stroke I was sitting beside her and we had just been talking

- she had a very good sense of humor. I think mine is good but hers was better.   Her sense of humour would put mine to shame.

For women, I think our health issues are tied up with our financial issues because we tend to live longer, and the level of care we'll have in the end is dependent upon our finances.

Of course it is. My sister's husband had an import/export business and he left her comfortable. And just about a year and a half ago or so, she sold his business. She said, "I think I'll sell this now because if I should take sick and I have to be in a nursing home I can pay my way." I remember saying to her that she inherited some of this sense from mother. She was in a nursing home and even though she wasn't there that long, it still was $2,000 a month. She had the best of care and she didn't have to worry because the money was there to take care it. Although I know her boys would have come together for her, but she was sort of an independent person.

As a head nurse, you were responsible for budgeting. But I wonder if the nursing environment or the camaraderie you had allowed for the discussion of finances?

Every Wednesday morning we had an in-service meeting from 7:30 to 8:30 and it could be on any topic. It was a chance for the staff to get together for an hour to voice whatever was on their minds. Sometimes they also had speakers in, and it worked out very well. Possibly I wasn't aware of it at the time, but it must have been that people felt comfortable talking to me.   They knew that if they said anything to me in confidence, it would never be repeated.

I remember I happened to be at lunch one day and I knew that the union and the nurses association were having an upset because of salaries. They wanted an increase and they didn't think they were going to get the increment they wanted. Six of them were sitting around talking about it. I was sitting there in the corner having my lunch and pretending I didn't hear their conversation because I'm on the other side of the fence, not that I would ever say anything about the people that were working with me. But they were going on about this and they couldn't see the forest for the trees. I had my lunch and finally I said, "Here you are, you're just squabbling over an increment – you must have this particular percentage." I said, "Did you ever stop to think how much this percentage is going to bring you monthly? Stop and think. If you get the amount you want, automatically it puts you in a higher tax bracket so you're going to pay more income tax." They responded, "Oh." Let's say it was eight percent. I said, "Instead of fighting for 8% go for 5% but ask for an extra week of vacation." They thought for a while and one said, "That makes sense." Suddenly the light came on. They said, "How come you're so smart?" I said, "I'm not that smart, just sensible. Isn't the time off better for you than giving the extra money you work for back to the Government?" That was the road they took. When you're not right in a situation you can be more level-headed about it. They didn't get the percentage they wanted but they got the extra week. I said afterwards, "Another week's vacation with full pay – that's money."

You must have worked long hours?

Regular hours. I was always there early in the morning but most of the time I would be off when I was supposed to be. But then I would be at home and the phone would ring. Even if you decided you had to work late, as a manager you didn't get paid for overtime, so you'd do it because it's the love of the job. Some people call you at home on your time because they want to make a decision and they want to make the right decision.

Was retirement an adjustment for you?

Not really, because when I've decided I'm going to do something I do it, and I never look back. I've always been able to do that, I move on. Travel was really the thing for me. Then I got involved with the board here at the condo. When I was working full time I was the president here and when I retired, I got pulled in even more. Then a year later I was getting calls from the hospital asking if I wanted to come back to do some part-time work. And there are two nursing homes close by to my home and both of them called me. I told them no, I am not going back to nursing because my days of nursing are over.

You've built up a nice nest egg. We could be having a follow-up discussion 20 years from now when you are 95. Did you think of leaving a legacy financially, was that part of your planning?

Not really, because I don't have children. I have two nieces and two nephews. My nieces are doing OK. They have very good educations and the older one is an Oxford graduate. The other one is a physiotherapist and now she has her own clinic. So I don't have to worry about them, they don't need me dishing it out.

Have you given any thought to your nineties, and if you had to move?

If I had to move from here, I would be able to. I think that I would have enough money to keep me wherever I wanted to go. That doesn't seem to worry me at all. I sort of live for today and whatever happens, happens.

So stress isn't a factor for you, you seem very relaxed.

When I was working, some days could be stressful, but it's no use flogging a dead horse. The stressful situation has passed so you move on. It's not time to sit down and worry about what's happened two hours ago. It's happened.

Lots of us dwell on stuff too long.

I know, and it's silly. It doesn't change anything. All it does is give you more grey hair and I already have enough of that. You know, I do remember a lecture from one of my professors. He was talking about stress, and he said that a bit of stress in everyone's life is good. He said we couldn't get along without it. But when stress becomes distress, sit up and take notice. It's true and I've always remembered that. I've said it to so many people, to so many youngsters.

That's a little gem of advice. What other gems do you have for me?

Oh dear, I can't think of any at the moment but I'm always throwing them at people. I don't even think they are gems.

I have no regrets in my life. There is one thing that I missed in my life and that's not having children. I'm sorry that I never had children because I really love children. For some reason or other, children always come to me. I don't know what it is. It's really, really funny. I would have been a good mother. I would have been rather strict though.

It sounds like you would have been your mom.

Yes. It would have been very important for my children to get an education and to want to study. If they didn't want to study, we would have been bad friends.

165

The importance of education seems to be a theme in the interviews I've conducted for this book. I usually ask, "What one piece of advice would you give?" and women often reply, "Get a good education."

It's so important and you are never too old to say you are going to start. I knew a lady, a nurses' assistant, and she must have been in her forties. I was talking to her one day and she said, "I'm so sorry that I didn't go into nursing because now I realize my limitations." I said to her that she could enter nursing as an advanced student. I said, "If it is something you really want to do, go ahead and do it." She said, "Over the years I've been taking night classes and I've got caught up on this and I've got caught up on that." I said, "Well, go ahead and do it." And she did. She went to Toronto and she wrote me when she graduated. That made me feel so good. Here was a woman in her forties who went back to school and she did well. Those are the people who do very well. She knew what she wanted; she hit the books.

Did you get a lot of satisfaction from your work?

I never was unhappy about going to work, even when it was snowing out there really bad!

And you have a wonderful sense of self-confidence. Did you always have that?

I think it came over time. Respect is something that if you give it, you get it. Self-confidence is something I think you develop. I could say something to a person, and be almost firm, but never impolite. I could be firm with you, but you would never be able to say that I was impolite to you. Just put yourself in the other person's place.

Here's an example, I remember when I was at the Civic we had a surgeon with a very short fuse, and he insisted on having an assistant. I didn't think it was necessary, he didn't really need an assistant because all he was doing was removing someone's toenail. Not a big thing, you could do that in the office. It was a busy evening, and he wanted to know, "Who's in charge here" and blah, blah, blah. He was jumping up and down, so I said to him, "Doctor, if you would stop jumping up and down like a yo-yo and say what you want, you will get served much faster." It went all over the theatre [operating room] that I had spoken to this man that nobody ever dared say anything to. And do you know, as a result of my saying that to him we became the best of friends. He went on the floor and told the nurses that I had told him off.

He was Mr. Diefenbaker's surgeon. [John Diefenbaker was Canada's 13th Prime Minister]. Then Mr. Diefenbaker arrived in the OR. I was working afternoons and Mr. Diefienbaker was going to have surgery on a Saturday morning. The surgeon insisted that he didn't want anybody else there in the OR for Mr. Diefenbaker but me: I had to be there. The surgeon introduced us. Mr Diefenbaker was having surgery under local anesthetic and I stood at the head of the table and I was talking to him and we became good friends, and he wrote letters to me afterwards. The morning of the surgery, the surgeon said to Mr Diefenbaker, "This is the nurse that I was telling you about, that put me in my place." I said, "Oh no, that is not true, I would never do that." He said, "You'd never do that? You did it!"

I thought that being in management …

At that time, I wasn't in management. That is what had everybody so shook up. Here was this staff nurse telling off this doctor who nobody, but nobody crossed. You had to

167

laugh, it had everybody in stitches. And, the supervisor, she found out about it too and she said, "You did something that I wanted to do for years." I said, "Well why didn't you?" She said, "I'm not a diplomat like you. You can get away with it."

What I'm finding when I speak to women about their financial empowerment or their financial success, is that it comes out of other characteristics. There is no way, I think, you can be financially self-sufficient without having some level of self-confidence.

When I was much younger, I was kind of shy but I got over that in a hurry.

Like a bad case of the measles right?

Why would I make myself and other people miserable? Does it get you anywhere? I can't get any more grey hair than I already have.

Chapter Eighteen

Investment & Insurance Choices

> "The life of every man is a diary in which he means to write one story, and writes another; and his humblest hour is when he compares the volume as it is with what he hoped to make it."
>
> Sir James Matthew Barrie, Scottish dramatist and author

Financial independence is most closely associated with retirement. In my practice, clients ask, "When can I retire?" I think retirement is a misnomer. What clients are really asking is, "When can I live off my investments?" The answer is different for everyone. We establish or secure our standard of living tomorrow by how we spend and save our money today. But the odds are that if we do not save and invest regularly, we will not retire comfortably.

I'd like to make an important point about being single and financial planning, and that is: it's one of life's realities. If you are not single now, you were in the past and may be again. Statistics Canada says that females age 70 have a 31% chance of living to age 90. And most people who are 90 or older are single. Therefore, whether you planned on living that long or not, for some portion of your adult life you are single. Financially there are pluses and minuses to being single, just as there are for other circumstances in life. On the minus side of the equation, your expenses are greater when they are not shared. But on the plus side, it's your money and you get to decide how you spend it. And there is no greater feeling than having control over your own money. After all, we want to experience some level of financial independence, don't we?

Investing

Now we come to the topic of investing. This is the hardest part of the book to write, but in some ways it will be the easiest because it's going to be a relatively short section. I cannot begin to tell you everything there is to know about investing, not in one sitting, not in one book. And the truth of the matter is that, even as a professional, it is very tough to stay on top of every new financial product out there – the investing landscape changes daily.

I can tell you this. It is important to recognize your comfort zone; it's important not to be intimidated but to use your common sense. It's also important to address investing questions and decisions and to do your homework. At this point, I think we have agreed that we're not going to be able to survive on saved grocery money, we will need larger assets which we have managed and acted responsibly towards. We need to be investing, and we need to approach the world of investing by being open to new knowledge and new concepts but tempering our enthusiasm for "getting rich" with a realistic view of our own situation.

There are two basic ways we invest. We either lend our money and receive interest payments for having allowed someone else to borrow our money. Or we purchase something of value, which we think will increase in value, so that we can sell it to somebody else and receive more money than we originally paid.

There are a number of ways we can lend our money. We can lend our money to the Government of Canada by purchasing Canada Savings Bonds. We can lend our money to a bank by purchasing a Guaranteed Investment Certificate (GIC). We can lend our money to an individual company by purchasing a corporate bond. Or we can lend our money to a number of governments (federal, provincial, municipal) and a number of companies, by investing in a bond mutual fund. The manager of the bond mutual fund uses our money, as well as everyone else's deposits, to buy government and corporate bonds on our behalf.

These types of investments are referred to as fixed income investments. When we receive interest payments from these investments we are receiving income. And to some degree we know what kind of income to expect in the form of a percentage. We know that if a one-year GIC is paying 3%, at the end of one year we will receive interest which represents 3% of the original amount we loaned to the bank where we purchased the GIC. The income amount is, in this case, fixed. The bank had the opportunity to use our money for a year and in "thanks" it paid us 3%. Not all fixed income investments have guaranteed rates of return. For some, the return will fluctuate depending on how the investment has been structured. But in general we have a fair idea of what our rate of return will be. We must also remember that in Canada if we earn interest income outside of a tax-sheltered vehicle, i.e. outside of our RRSP or registered retirement income fund (RRIF) it will be taxed at the highest income tax rate applicable to each of us, just like employment or pension income.

When we purchase something of value in the hopes of it being worth more one day, when we will turn around and resell it, we are purchasing an asset. Property is an asset. We can purchase property in the form of "real property" i.e. a home, a cottage, or a piece of land. Or we can purchase property in the form of a stock, which means we own a fraction of a company. Many people buy stocks in individual companies. For some it is an investment, for others it is a gamble. When you make money after selling a stock, you won't pay as much tax as if you had made the same amount of money in interest income. That is because currently interest income is 100% taxable, whereas the gain on an investment, referred to as a capital gain, is only 50% taxable.

In other words, when you or I buy a stock, or a mutual fund whose underlying investments are stocks, and we sell our investment receiving more money than we originally paid, we have a gain only half of which is taxable. The other half we get to keep free and clear without paying income tax on it. There are really only two investments/assets which are completely tax free in Canada: the gain on our principal residence (your house, condo, or in some cases your cottage) and the proceeds from a life insurance policy with a named beneficiary.

'Stocks,' 'shares' and 'equities' are words which are often used interchangeably. Many Canadians who own stocks have made their purchases via a mutual fund. Mutual funds can invest in bonds and/or they can invest in stocks. Each of us is so busy with our own jobs and lives, that we don't have the time to properly research individual companies to decide if and when we should buy or sell their stocks. Therefore, we leave this decision to a fund manager. He or she makes those decisions on behalf of every person who deposits money into the mutual fund.

If we don't have the time, information or capabilities to research on an ongoing basis every potential decision to be made with respect to buying and selling stocks, then the stock purchases we do make are more likely to fall on the

172

gambling side of the equation. However, if we purchase units in a mutual fund, then essentially we've hired a money manager. It is the full-time job of the money manager to do the research and to make the appropriate choices. In that case, our purchase is much more likely to be an investment.

Keep in mind that mutual funds can be as diverse as the stock markets themselves. Mutual funds can be very conservative, investing only in government bonds for example, or they can be very aggressive, and therefore volatile, investing only in emerging companies within emerging markets. Mutual funds cover the spectrum on the "conservative to aggressive" volatility scale. You will want to know what the mutual fund invests in and its history before you invest. A CFP can give you advice in this area.

Probably your first investment, as it was for all of us, was some kind of piggy bank or a wallet. Then you opened your first bank account. At the bank you learned about certificates of deposit or GICs. At some point, either from your bank, or exposure to media and advertising, or in discussion with family or friends, you learned about other investments, such as stocks and bonds, mutual funds, insurance products, etc.

It makes sense that our investment choices are progressive and hopefully methodical. We learn as we go. And there is nothing like making mistakes and learning the hard way. That's perfectly normal. You need to be open to new information and new knowledge. You also need to check-in with yourself as you progress. As you make different investment choices, you will come to know your comfort level regarding risk and volatility. This is important – it's okay to take some risk and to be a bit nervous with the amount of risk you're taking. Life itself offers no guarantees, so it seems pretty silly to expect that all investment choices made over our lifetime will be totally risk-free and fully guaranteed. That's not realistic. Worthwhile endeavors put us on a learning curve and require us to stretch.

Turn your investment choices into educated choices. Does a specific investment make inherent sense – does it involve common sense? The world is in flux; your investment choices need to make sense in a fluctuating world with fluctuating markets and economies. Does it work with your big picture? Do you understand this investment or do you need to learn more? What's the most you could lose? What's the most you could gain? Are you comfortable with this range? Gambling is luck, pure and simple, but investing is informed risk-taking. The way we make "risk" a less scary concept, is by having confidence in our ability to learn, assimilate information, put it in perspective, and then make changes as we go.

It's impossible to know it all, to know everything there is to know every second of every day. (As if you needed me to remind you of that.) You only need to ask: "Does this investment choice make sense for me at this time?" If you have given yourself room to maneuver, and your strategy incorporates flexibility, then you'll be okay. These are the guidelines I recommend.

You will be learning constantly. For example, the flip-side of every investment decision is taxation. And while taxes and death are two of life's certainties, how we are taxed isn't always certain, it can change. Even if the structure of taxation isn't changing, the make-up or composition of your income could, which means you will want to go back and review what you are doing and perhaps make revised investment decisions.

Another word about taxation, although income tax was to be a temporary measure to help the country get through World War One, it is not going to go away. And some people believe that once they retire they shouldn't have to pay taxes any more. That's not realistic either. Nobody wants to pay more tax than they have to, and everyone has the right to set up their affairs in as tax efficient a manner as possible. We also have the right to express our views when we don't like how various levels of government are spending our tax dollars. It is important to understand how we are taxed individually, but once we've saved as much tax as we can, then we also need to stand back and look at the advantages our tax contributions generate.

We must never forget how lucky we are to live in this country. We can take pride in our standard of living. The taxes each of us pays makes life better for all Canadians. It wouldn't take long to begin a lengthy list of the many ways we benefit from the services our tax dollars provide – our beautiful parks is the first item to come to my mind. I guess what I am trying to say is, we ought to smile when we pay our taxes. We're very fortunate indeed to be in a position to pay income tax – if nothing else, it means that we have an income. (Remember, I mentioned earlier that your financial planner would say things you don't want to hear?)

"Understand this, my friends: Every dream in life has a financial price, just as every action you take and every decision you make has an economic consequence. To get where you want to go, you must figure out what those costs are."

Georgette Mosbacher, *It Takes Money, Honey*

There are many, many books out there that deal with the nuts and bolts of financial planning issues, and in lots of detail. A list of currently available books, which I am recommending appears at the end of this chapter. It is a partial list of the many "personal finance" books on the market, and I favour Canadian authors such as Tim Cestnick and Gail Vaz-Oxlade. Take your time in choosing books and do some browsing if you can. The fit of the book will depend on your current knowledge and interest. Try to stay away from anything that looks like hype or scare tactics. You will want to read more than one book, but take it one book at a time, so you don't become overwhelmed, and give yourself time to absorb what you are reading.

You may also begin looking at the "money" section in large daily papers or you can go online and read articles from newspapers in other metropolitan areas. Large newspapers tend to have a "business" section which can be intimidating if you are getting your feet wet in the world of investing. But they often have a "money" section, usually on the weekend or as a supplement. That is where you can find lots of good information, because the articles are user-friendly and specifically geared to personal financial matters as opposed to the business world on a global scale.

With everything you read, always ask yourself, does this make sense for me? Is that something I need to be concerned about now? Is this helping me to become empowered or am I starting to feel paranoid and panicky? Stick with the empowering stuff, because the panicky, fearful stuff is a dime a dozen. You will always find financial planning material that can scare or confuse the heck out of you, and which isn't very helpful, so be discerning and use common sense. No one knows you better than you.

> **"Money management may look like a science, but unlike physics or chemistry, there are no immutable laws to guide us when it comes to investing."**
>
> Gail Vaz-Oxlade, *Chatelaine July 2001*

You might consider looking into a financial planning course offered through the adult education department of high schools in your area or through community colleges. I've been asked to teach such a course for women at a community college here in Ottawa – what a great course to be able to offer. Discussion is generated because everyone is made to feel comfortable and confidentiality is respected. It's as though we we're sitting at one big kitchen table. Each person is there to learn at least one new thing, and when you are in a supportive, interactive group you can't help but root for each other. There may be some like-minded women in your community or circle of friends who would be interested in establishing an informal setting where you can invite financial professionals to speak and share a cup of coffee. I have fond memories of speaking at the Women's Institute in Jasper, Ontario (yes, there is a Jasper, Ontario) and at the National Capital Region Chapter of Canadian Women in Communication. Your group doesn't have to be formal; the atmosphere needs to be relaxed and the participants genuinely interested. When you have that kind of setting you get great questions, and sometimes we learn more from the questions others ask than the ones we ask. If you have discussion, questions and laughter, then you have education, inspiration and empowerment.

I encourage you to go off and learn about some of the many different types of investments out there, and learn about which ones are right for you from all resources available: newspapers, books, the internet, courses, seminars, and people you trust. Those resources alone could have you studying all day.

As a foundation, you will want to learn about the pros & cons of different types of investments, what sort of histories they have, and how they are affected by taxation. As you make your investment choices maintain flexibility, be prepared to make some mistakes and know that the world will throw you curve balls along the way. Change and adaptation are part of the game. To help put things in perspective, here's a list of some of the milestones we've lived through over the last half of the last century of investing. (My thanks to Anthony Di Meo & Dexter Robinson of Andex Associates Inc. – see www.andexcharts.com)

1950: A Canadian stamp was 4 cents
1951: The life expectancy for men was 66 1/2 years and for women 71 years. Just under 8% of the Canadian population was over age 65.
1952: Old Age Security started for those reaching age 70
1956: The Dow Jones Industrial Average closed above 500
1957: RRSPs had their start with a limit of $2,500
1964: Minimum wage in Canada was $1.00
1965: The Canada Pension Plan was approved.
Old Age Security was reduced from age 70 to 65
1968: Canada's first lottery had a $100,000 prize
1970: Canada and the US were in a recession
1972: The Dow Jones Industrial Average closed above 1000
1973: Average family income in Canada was $12,716
1974: The Toronto Stock Exchange 300 closed above 1000
1976: Minimum wage was now $2.90 and the RRSP limit rose to $5,500
1979: Canada's first gold coin, The Maple Leaf, went on sale
1981: Interest rates peaked at 21%

1982: Canada and the US were in a recession
1985: Average family income in Canada was $38,059
1986: The Toronto Stock Exchange 300 closed above 3000
1987: The Dow Jones Industrial Average closed above 2000
1989: The Canada and US Free Trade agreement was
approved
1991: The Goods & Services Tax (GST) started
1992: The RRSP limit rose to $12,500
1995: The life expectancy for men had increased to 75
years, and for women to 81 years
1997: Average family income in Canada was $57,146
The minimum wage was now $6.85
1999: Over 12% of the Canadian population was now over
age 65
2000: The Dow Jones Industrial Average hit 11,908
The Toronto Stock Exchange 300 hit 11,325
A Canadian stamp was 47 cents + GST

We can see that stock markets are volatile. The reason dollar-cost-averaging (having a regular amount deposited into your investments on a regular basis) is successful is due to market volatility. Still it is hard to see our own investments be "down" at any point in time. But the markets aren't personal. If your basket of investments is balanced and diversified, and its value is currently down, then you can be assured that every other Canadian with a similar portfolio is down at the same time, and up at the same time as you are. As you educate yourself you will become more understanding of risk and volatility with respect to investing over time. And the more you learn about how you are taxed and how much you are taxed, the more confident you will feel in your choices.

Insurance

I am a firm believer in insurance. However, just like investing, we have an equally large number of options when it comes to insurance. And just as our investment needs will shift between our 20's and our 60's and beyond, the same is true for our insurance needs. You will learn as you go and your knowledge in this area, like so many others, will be cumulative. Please be reassured that it is good to acquire knowledge cumulatively - that's how we develop wisdom.

Here are some points to consider. I believe all adults have a need for basic life insurance coverage: a lump sum amount that will be paid out at death. If you pass away and you are single with no dependents, but you have an apartment, a car lease, some belongings, and some outstanding student debt, then you have a need for insurance. If you die and you are a parent, single or married, with a mortgage, dreams for your child's education and perhaps parents who are still alive, then you need life insurance. If you are lucky enough to die when you are elderly, but at that time you will leave an elderly spouse, or an adult child who may have a difficult time coping in the world due to a physical impairment or mental health concerns, your family will benefit from insurance.

Life insurance with a named beneficiary, pays out within weeks of your death upon completion of the claim form and the provision of the death certificate. Why is this important? Because there are immediate financial needs at your death. The truth is that the world does not stop turning when we die. All outstanding amounts at our death are still due. Bills need to be paid, both the regular kind such as payment of utilities and credit cards, as well as the exceptional obligations such as outstanding medical payments, for example your ambulance bill. There will be legal bills in the future and perhaps an accountant's bill too. There will be funeral expenses, even for a simple cremation. The people you leave behind in general, and your executor in particular (see the next chapter) need to have the financial resources readily available to be able to tidy up your affairs. Life insurance is a clean and simple way to fund immediate, final expenses.

A named beneficiary means that within the life insurance policy you have named a person (and it can be more than one person) to whom you wish to have the money paid at your death. You can name whom ever you want, but it should be an adult, not a minor child. The person you name will receive that money tax-free, which means that your estate doesn't pay any tax on the insurance benefit and the person who receives it does not declare the payment as income and therefore does not pay income tax on it either.

There are many, many different reasons why you would want to leave someone a lump sum amount of tax-free money at your death. And a lump sum amount of money doesn't mean millions of dollars. In fact you may have bought life insurance in the past and thought, "gosh that's a good chunk of money I'm leaving behind." But as time has passed the value of that benefit has lessened; the claim amount isn't worth as much as it used to be.

Here's an example of my own. Many years ago I bought a $50,000 life insurance policy. I wasn't married, I didn't have kids and I wasn't in debt. However, I could foresee that my mother would probably live into her 90's and one day she would become financially dependent, to some degree, on my brother, my sister and me. If I died prematurely, that would place a greater burden on my siblings who were married and raising families, to care for our mom financially in her old age. I could see that my mother was potentially a dependent and I wanted to provide for her and to assist my brother and sister. I thought I was being responsible and generous when I bought that policy and I was, but $50,000 today doesn't go nearly as far as it once did.

Today I'm married, and my husband is a colleague who, as part of the financial planning process, has been selling life insurance for over 25 years. I can tell you that when a client of Marc's has died and the surviving spouse has received money from a policy he sold them, the surviving spouse has never turned to Marc and asked him to take the money back. No widow or widower has said, "I wish I wasn't coming into this money. I don't need it and I can't use it. It isn't a help to me." Again, the idea isn't to create multi-millionaires at your death, it's to make life easier for the people who love you.

Life insurance products range from simple such as a "term 5" or "term 10" policy to complicated such as a Universal Life policy. The different types of insurance products each have their benefits, but again the question is what is best for you. There are interesting things you can do with insurance, from saving taxes, to creating a legacy, making a charitable donation, or providing for the intergenerational transfer of wealth. This book cannot tell you everything there is to know about insurance, but hopefully it will encourage you and empower you to explore your options.

Here are some key points to consider:

You need to purchase insurance when you don't need it. That's one of the hardest stumbling blocks for people when it comes to this product. You need to buy insurance when you are healthy or "insurable." Once an insurance policy is in place the insurance company cannot cancel the policy on you. If I buy insurance today, but develop ovarian cancer three years from now, the insurance company cannot cancel my policy because I've become a much greater risk to them and a potential liability. We have a contract. However, I can choose to cancel the policy at any time, basically by discontinuing my premium payments. Premiums are the payments I make to keep the insurance policy in force. My obligation is to be honest when completing the application and to make my regular payments. (Also, not to commit suicide within the first two years of owning the policy.) If I choose at some later date to cancel my policy or, more wisely, to replace it with a policy which is better suited to my changing needs, I have the right to do so.

Insurance is cheaper the younger and healthier you are. If you are a smoker your premiums (also called rates) will be almost double the rates of a non-smoker. The insurance company isn't making a moral statement by charging smokers higher rates. Their experience bears out the increased cost of insuring smokers. In other words, statistically a smoker will die sooner, which means the insurance company will be paying the claim within a shorter time frame and therefore, will not receive as many premium payments from the person who owns the policy.

This is also why the rates for men can be greater than the rates for women. Men statistically die sooner. Life insurance is not a scam. Think of it from the insurance companies' point of view. They are continually trying to assess the risk of individuals dying within a given time frame. We are all going to die – that's not the question, the question is when? And life insurance is a very competitive product. So an insurance company doesn't want to charge more than they have to, after all they want to attract you as a customer.

On the other hand, by producing a policy they have made a legally binding contract and they must charge enough in premiums to support future claims as well as the cost of running and maintaining the insurance company.

Also, in order to keep premium rates in line, the insurance company wants to know that it is starting with as healthy a pool of individuals as possible. Based on your age and the amount of insurance you are purchasing (i.e. the amount of risk the insurance company is assuming) you may have to answer some medical questions or have some medical tests completed before you qualify for coverage. Again this is why you want to purchase insurance sooner rather than later, and while you are healthy. Think of insurance as being on sale today as compared to tomorrow.

Some types of insurance are a better deal for some people than for other people, take mortgage insurance for example. If you hold your mortgage with a bank you may have purchased mortgage insurance. The beneficiary of this insurance is the bank. If you die, the bank doesn't have to worry about trying to get future mortgage payments from your estate or next of kin. The policy pays the balance owing on your mortgage to the bank. The bank has no worries and your surviving family can stay in the home mortgage-free. You pay for this benefit through your premiums which may be combined with your mortgage payments. Now if you're terribly out of shape or overweight, perhaps a smoker, or older with a family history of heart problems, this insurance could be a good deal. However, if you are in your twenties or early thirties, in great shape, with healthy parents and siblings, it may be less expensive for you to buy your own policy based on the individual risk you pose to the insurance company.

If you purchase individual insurance in our scenario above, the person you choose as the beneficiary could use the residual claim which isn't required to cover the mortgage. Let's say you buy $200,000 of life insurance because that's the amount currently owing on your home. Over time that amount owing will diminish. So if you pass away in 10 years time, the mortgage of less than $200,000 would be paid and the residual would be available for your partner's living expenses or for your children's education. What if you passed away and your partner or spouse didn't want to stay in the home – either for emotional reasons or for practical reasons? It is possible that without you bringing income into the household your partner would choose to move for professional opportunities or for childcare assistance? If you were living away from extended family or in a rural setting, that arrangement may no longer be practical for the new single-parent family. Or perhaps your spouse doesn't want to pay-off the mortgage at your death. Maybe you have a child who has a unique artistic talent or athletic ability, and your spouse would prefer to have the life insurance put towards special schooling or coaching that would allow your child to pursue his or her dream. By purchasing individual life insurance as opposed to mortgage insurance, you have given your family more flexibility.

I encourage you to explore your life insurance options in the same way that I encourage you to increase your investment knowledge; one step at a time. Deal with reputable companies, and meet with professionals who come recommended by people you respect. Don't feel pressured – it's your money. Make decisions. Know that you may have to revise your decisions and that possibly you will "make mistakes." But know that you are just as likely to make some very good and wise choices. My $50,000 life insurance policy may not have the same value it had when I bought it, but I'm glad I did. Hindsight is always 20/20. Back in the early 80's when interest rates were in the double-digits, as many people wished they had bought bonds, GICs or annuities (an insurance product) as those who wished they hadn't bought their first home and taken on a mortgage. Perhaps we no longer get to take advantage of double-digit interest rates, but then we are not living with double-digit inflation and mortgages either. There is more than one way to look at a financial challenge, or should I say opportunity?

> **"Pushing through fear is less frightening than living with the underlying fear that comes from a feeling of helplessness."**
>
> Susan Jeffers, *Feel the Fear and Do It Anyway*

Long-Term Disability

Here is some brief information on a few other types of insurance: Long-Term Disability, Critical Illness and Long-Term Care. Disability insurance provides you with an amount of money on a weekly or monthly basis, and this money is designed to replace the employment income you would lose by being disabled and unable to work. Disability insurance is not designed to fully replace employment income. Again, we need to think about it from the insurance company's point of view. If we could replace 100% of our income by being disabled, a lot of people would manage to become disabled very quickly and would find lots of reasons not to return to work. Disability is not retirement.

At the same time, it is easy to imagine how difficult our situation would truly be if we could not work because of a disability. We'd not only be unable to earn income, we would have larger medical expenses over a long period of time. Since we are more likely to become disabled at some point in our lives, than to simply die outright, this type of insurance is important and most large employers provide or offer disability insurance to their employees. Disability insurance purchased individually can be expensive. Like all other kinds of insurance you can purchase a very simple policy, or one with all the bells and whistles attached. (Bells and whistles are called "riders" in the insurance industry.)

Depending on when you became disabled, the insurance company may not receive many years of premium but could potentially be paying the claim amount for many years to come. Unlike life insurance, a disability claim is not a one-time payment. By participating through a group plan at work the risk is shared or pooled and as result the premiums can be lowered – the larger the size of the group the less likely that all its members will become disabled. However, disability insurance is a real concern for those who are self-employed. Consider small business owners, or service providers such as accountants, lawyers, doctors, dentists, vets, etc. Not only do they generate income to support their families, but also their employees are dependent on their ability to work. Rent, equipment, inventory and utilities still need to be paid. So while disability coverage may appear to be costly, the cost of not having appropriate insurance coverage could be much, much worse.

Critical Illness

What about stay-at-home parents? If they became disabled, especially permanently, the effects of disability could be equally devastating for their families, including the financial effects. Yet they do not qualify for disability insurance because they do not receive income. You have to earn verifiable income in order to put a policy in place to replace it. Luckily, there is a type of insurance called critical illness. While it wasn't designed with stay-at-home parents in mind, it can provide some peace of mind in the face of a life-altering diagnosis.

Critical illness insurance was originally designed to provide financial assistance to the victims of heart attacks. With improved medicine and surgery, one doesn't automatically die of a heart attack any more, but one's life could be permanently altered. Critical illness coverage is somewhat similar to life insurance in that you purchase a lump sum amount to be received tax-free, if you are diagnosed with a life-threatening disease or life-altering condition. And like life insurance, you need to buy it when you don't need it; it's also less expensive the younger and healthier you are. I have critical illness coverage. If I am diagnosed with ovarian cancer as in the example earlier, or any of the other sixteen debilitating conditions listed in my policy, the amount I have purchased will be paid to me, tax-free, to use as I wish.

As the claimant, you get to decide how you want to spend the money resulting from a critical illness claim – the money is yours. You could use it to supplement your income, re-fit or renovate your home, or to seek medical treatment in another province or country. It could be used to cover nursing costs, childcare costs, mortgage or debt payments. Maybe you would choose to take that once-in-a-lifetime trip to Paris that you've always dreamed about.

Obviously, this is an area of insurance which is becoming more and more popular the longer we live. I see it as an important complement to life insurance.

*These are the conditions covered by my
Critical Illness policy:*

Heart Attack
Stroke
Life-Threatening Cancer
Coronary Artery Bypass
Kidney Failure
Blindness
Major Organ Transplant
Alzheimer's Disease
Parkinson's Disease
Paralysis
Multiple Sclerosis
Deafness
Loss of Speech
Coma
Severe Burns
Loss of Limbs
Occupational HIV

Long-Term Care

Another relatively new and increasingly popular form of insurance is Long-Term Care. Long-Term Care provides tax-free money on a weekly basis which is used to cover the cost of care when we can no longer perform certain basic functions of living. We may require care due to illness or an accident, or we may need assistance because of deteriorating physical or mental abilities as we age. This is exactly what Long-Term Care was designed for. Under most policies you qualify to make a claim when you require assistance in performing two or more activities of daily living.

189

These activities are:

Bathing
Dressing
Eating
Toileting
Continence
Transferring (moving to or from a bed or a chair)

You can choose to pay a family member, a friend, or a professional to assist you, and you can receive the benefits whether you are in your home, in a care facility such as a nursing home, or receiving adult day care.

You can imagine how many people born after 1950 could potentially benefit from this kind of insurance: the aging boomers – gosh we're tired of that term aren't we? But the truth of the matter is that not only are we living longer, and therefore needing more care in our frailer years, but our children are living longer too. Will they really be in a position to help us? Is it realistic to rely on your children? I have a dear, sweet client who is 88 years old. She has outlived her husband and two of her three children. Her surviving daughter is in her sixties and has more health problems than her mom. My client's doctor has told her that she needs to consider moving from her apartment into a retirement or nursing home. Who will help my client research her options, assist her with the move, and help her give away or dispose of the items she can't take with her? But above all else, who will help her financially and provide for the care she might need ten years from now? My client is not wealthy, nor can she buy Long-Term Care insurance. It's too late for her.

Please note: Insurance doesn't just involve planning. Insurance involves pre-planning!

I have confidence in your ability to learn about those areas of insurance and investing which are relevant to you. I'm not trying to add to your workload or to your stress level, by sending you off on this mission. These topics can be complicated, but to ignore them can put your quality of life in jeopardy. Use your common sense and filter the information you will come across.

Two nights ago on TV, I saw a small news item about a woman celebrating her 108th birthday. She was dainty, nicely dressed and groomed, with her family gathered around her. With her arthritic hands she joined in the clapping as the camera showed the cake that would feed her well-wishers. She had a look on her face which suggested she knew she'd be doing this again next year when everyone would be back, including the TV crew reporting on her 109th birthday. She had that "life is strange" look. Perhaps she knew it could just as easily have been different for her. Who knows in her 108 years how often she'd had a brush with death or disability, either because of illness or an accident? How many of her friends and family, much younger than herself, have predeceased her? And if I had sat down with her as a financial planner, when she was 68, and said "we needed to review your investment strategy and look at saving you taxes, because you still have another 40 years of living to fund," do you think she would have thought I was crazy?

Life is strange. We can't control it, but we can be better prepared by being realistic and addressing issues such as incapacity and premature death, as well as longevity and frailty. Rather than being our own worst enemies when it comes to financial planning, we have the ability to become our own best friends.

191

Why, since I've never had any intention
Of going out on the street and selling my body,
Is it hard to be reaching an age where
I won't find a buyer?

From *"Twenty Questions"* by Judith Viorst

Recommended Books (*www.chapters.indigo.ca*)

Author	Title	Publisher	ISBN #
Bach, David	*Smart Couples Finish Rich: Canadian ed.*	Doubleday Canada 2003	0385659660
Cestnick, Tim	*Winning the Estate Planning Game 2001*	Prentice Hall Canada, 2001	013028517X
Cestnick, Tim	*Winning the Tax Game 2003*	Viking Press, 2002	0670043338
Chilton, David	*The Wealthy Barber Gold Edition*	Financial Awareness Group 2002	0968394736
Foster, Sandra E.	*You Can't Take it With You*	John Wiley & Sons 2002	0470831561
Jacks, Evelyn	*Tax Savings for the Long Run*	McGraw-Hill Ryerson 2002	0070894531
Leatherdale, Linda	*Money is a Girl's Best Friend*	Turnerbooks 1998	1552280144
Martin, Tony & Eric Tyson	*Personal Finance For Canadians for Dummies, 3rd ed.*	Wiley – Inter science 2001	1894413296
Roseman, Ellen	*Money 101*	John Wiley & Sons 2003	0470832363
Thomas Yaccato, Joanne	*Balancing Act*	Pearson Education Canada 1999	0130860514
Vaz-Oxlade, Gail	*A Woman of Independent Means*	Stoddart Publishing 1999	0773731857
Vaz-Oxlade, Gail	*Divorce: A Canadian Woman's Guide*	Pearson Education Canada 2002	0130265349

Chapter Nineteen

Wills and Powers of Attorney

The truth of the matter is, it's cheaper to die with a will than without one. And no member of your family is ever going to thank you if you die without a will.

All adults in our society, under our customs of laws, should have this document properly written. A will is a legal declaration. In Canada, wills fall under provincial legislation, but this section addresses topics which are universal to estate planning regardless of the jurisdiction in which you live. Whether your net worth ends in two zeros or seven zeros, someone will have to tidy things up when you die. Most people in their early 20's feel they don't need a will because they don't have dependents and they don't believe they have any assets. But even if you are single, you likely have debts and you definitely have a body, and both of these matters need to be handled.

The person or persons you choose to delegate this task to are called your executors (and may also be referred to as the trustee, personal representative or executrix if she is female, just to make things more complicated). An executor is responsible for acting upon the directions of a will. Below is a partial and potential list of the duties of an executor. Your executor's actual duties are dependent on your circumstances at the time of death. If you die young, you may have debts and obligations for example, outstanding credit cards, a car lease or loan, a mortgage or apartment lease, even student loans to be paid. If you die in old age you could have outstanding medical expenses and your executor may be dealing with the administrators of your nursing home, or he or she may be retrieving your body from your retirement place in Florida or Mexico.

When you die, regardless of your age, your remains become the property and responsibility of your executor. You might want to stipulate in your will how you wish to have your remains disposed of. Personally, I believe we are so much more than our bodies, and the good we do in this world has a rippling effect which lasts longer than our bodies ever could. However I don't find it difficult to discuss terms such as "remains" and "disposal" because that is the reality of dealing with organic matter. While we are more than just our bodies, we are also our bodies. Our bodies are the organic vessel for this journey here on earth. Sometimes it's hard to be as accepting of death as we are of birth. We are much more comfortable talking about the miracle of birth than we are about the mystery of death.

"Time does not become sacred to us until we have lived it, until it has passed over us and taken with it a part of ourselves."
John Burroughs, author and naturalist

If you die without a will, which is called dying intestate, then you don't have an executor and the courts will have to appoint someone to carry out your missing executor's tasks. This is time-consuming and potentially quite costly for your estate. Also, this could be very hard on your family. While the courts may go ahead and appoint a family member to take responsibility for your affairs, it may not be the family member you would have chosen.

I'd like to give you an example of how important this legal document, an updated will is. Before I worked as a Certified Financial Planner, I worked for a large Human Resources consulting firm and one of my tasks was the administration of employee benefits for a sizeable group of retirees. An early retiree and his wife went grocery shopping on a Saturday morning and they didn't come home. They were killed in a car accident. The retiree had a group life insurance policy and I acted as the liaison between the executor and the insurance company which would pay-out the claim. Because the named beneficiary was the wife and she had also died in the car accident, the insurance company asked for a copy of the autopsy reports in order to adjudicate the claim.

The executor sent me the autopsy reports but before I forwarded them on to the insurance company, I read them. I had never seen an autopsy report and I was curious. To this day I don't know if I should have read them but I'm glad I did. The ruling came back that one of the occupants of the car died half an hour before the other one and therefore the claim would be made payable to the heirs of the person who died last. I knew this was incorrect. Both the husband and wife had been burned to death in that accident, and based on the report, the fire had been instantaneous. What had happened was that one autopsy was performed half an hour before the other. The claim adjudicator misunderstood the times and obviously hadn't read the reports, mistaking the times of the autopsy for the times of death. Why was this important? Because it was a second marriage.

Both the husband and wife had children from their first marriages. So if the insurance company ruled that the husband had died earlier, the insurance money would have passed through his wife's estate to her heirs, her children. If they had ruled that she had pre-deceased him then the insurance monies would have passed to his heirs and stayed in his family. This situation could have had huge financial consequences for two different families. I advised the insurance company that they ought to go back and read the reports.

I want to point out that I have nothing against that particular insurance company, which was a large multi-national firm, not a fly-by-night operation. The incorrect adjudication came down to human error, which occurs in all industries.

But the real moral of the story is the following: because this couple had updated wills there was an executor to handle their situation. They still had a son at home, I believe he was in his late teens, and you can imagine what sort of a position or state he would have been in if there hadn't been an executor to step in. The second point I want to stress is that their wills were reflective of their circumstances and took into account that they were truly a blended family. So even if I hadn't caught the insurance company's error, their wills would have made sure there was an equitable distribution of the insurance proceeds as well as the other assets they owned.

Here are some points to consider when preparing to have your will and powers of attorney completed:

❑ I believe your will is far too important a document not to have it drawn up by a lawyer whose practice regularly includes estate issues. I'm often asked what I think about the "lawyer-approved" legal will kits you hear advertised on radio & TV. More than one estate lawyer has separately said to me that they make money when people don't fill-in those kits properly – and you will never know you didn't get it right. You can still buy preformatted, fill-in-the-blank, documents at stationery or office supply stores. But if you buy a kit, and your family has questions about what you completed, after you die, the cashier who rang in your will kit purchase won't be able to help them. At your death your family will probably have to see a lawyer, so it might as well be the lawyer who knew you, understood your intentions and made sure your legal documents were reflective of your wishes.

❑ If you don't know a lawyer, start asking friends if they've worked with a lawyer specifically regarding wills and estates. Especially helpful could be friends or colleagues who've recently had a death in their own family and who may have had dealings with a lawyer who was helpful and efficient. Referrals are the best place to start. Phone the lawyer's office and ask questions about the services provided and the associated costs. The treatment you receive on the phone will give you an indication of the atmosphere in the office. If you are planning to work with a Certified Financial Planner, he or she should be able to refer you to more than one lawyer with whom other clients have been happy to work.

❑ Prepare to meet with your lawyer. Give some thought to who will be your executor(s), who will be the guardian of children, who will be your beneficiaries. Make sure you have the correct and full spelling of each person's name. Have notes as well as questions written down. You don't have to have everything figured out before you meet, as your lawyer will give you suggestions on how best to structure your will. His or her advice will be based on their experience and the specific details you provide about you and your family. Give the particulars some preliminary thought. Remember your children are considered dependents but could your parents potentially be dependent on you? Also, bring a copy of your Net

199

Worth Statement; it's better to be over-prepared than under-prepared.

□ Your powers of attorney are as important as your will. We are six times more likely to become disabled than to die out right. So if you are in a coma in the hospital, in other words you are completely incapacitated but not dead, your executor can't carry out your wishes because he or she has no power to act on your behalf. And if you are in a coma it's too late to have your powers of attorney drawn up. These documents, just like your will, have to be in place before you need them.

□ In Ontario, for example, we have two powers of attorney. One for Property decisions which includes the handling of all financial matters i.e. paying your bills, making your retirement savings contribution, filing your tax return etc. And one for medical or Health Care decisions. You do not have to name the same person for both powers of attorney, and in fact you may not want to. Ultimately you want to choose people who will be able to function well or who will know how to handle certain aspects of your situation if something tragically happens to you. You want to choose people who will be effective, who will be business-like, detail-oriented, also calm and considerate.

You would want to choose a power of attorney for Health Care decisions who can handle being in a hospital or nursing home environment, who will be comfortable asking the appropriate questions of medical staff and who will be empathetic to the quality of life you would want to have. You want to choose a power of attorney for Property decisions who recognizes the importance of having matters dealt with and who would be able to step in and understand how you have arranged your affairs. In other words, you don't want to choose your "cousin

Terry" to be responsible for having your taxes completed and filed when "cousin Terry" can't seem to get his or her own taxes done on time.

❑ In the case of your powers of attorneys and your executor, I recommend that you name an alternate for each role. If you are in an accident, and your power of attorney is on a sailboat somewhere in the Greek islands, it makes sense to have a back-up. My other strong recommendation is that you ask the people you have chosen if they would be willing to fulfill those roles before you have your legal documents completed. Some people choose a family member because they feel it is a sign of respect or honour. But these roles could require a great deal of personal time and they come with a high degree of responsibility. So if your older brother is the father of triplets under the age of four, and he already feels he's away from home too much because of work, he may not see it as an honour to be your power of attorney or executor. Be honest and realistic in your choices.

Once you have your documents drawn up, your executors and powers of attorneys need to know where to access these as well as other papers and information. It doesn't make sense to pay a lawyer to have your will properly completed then lock it in a safety deposit box, if no one knows you have a safety deposit box, let alone the name of your lawyer or where the key is kept. Likewise, insurance companies are probably sitting on millions of dollars worth of claims, which should be paid out because the person insured has died, but no one knew their parents or grandparents owned these policies.

This is especially true when an older person passes away. In our society our elderly may have moved a number of times in their latter years: from their matrimonial home, to a smaller home or apartment, to a retirement home, perhaps to a convalescent home and then to a nursing home. When the move is to downsize, important papers including old insurance policies can easily get lost, as items are given away or destroyed. Another consideration is that sometimes we hide things of value. We've all put something away in a "safe place" at one time or another, and then can't remember where that safe place was. With time, an older person may have forgotten they even owned an insurance policy, and they will have no memory of where it could be now.

Are you a power of attorney or executor for someone else? In particular, for your spouse? Have you and your spouse talked about the consequences of an accident or death and the decisions that would need to be made and the actions to be taken. I'm not suggesting that this be the topic of conversation whenever you go out for a nice dinner, but if you haven't given some thought to estate planning and the logistics of being left alone suddenly, you leave yourself open to be swayed by the opinions and advice of those around you. And no matter how well meaning their advice, you are the one who must live with the decisions, including financial decisions, made at the time of a partner's death.

Buy yourself time and give some thought to this now. How exactly would you cope? What exactly would you do if your partner became injured or passed away? It's important to know that you can cope; that you would know who to contact and about what. That you would know what needed to be dealt with and in what order; that you could prioritize.

I remember reading about one of the widows of September 11th, 2001. She was a stay-at-home mom, accomplished and intelligent. However, when she lost her husband in the World Trade Center she also lost all their family records, because he had managed the family's finances from his computer and desk at work. Every bill, statement, record and file was gone. Which left her trying to put the pieces together, while being there emotionally for her children and the other grieving members of their family.

Here is a listing of some of the **Duties of an Executor:**

❑ The executor must find the will and read it.

❑ The executor is responsible for the remains and disposal of the deceased's body. He or she will be dealing with medical personnel and a funeral home, as well as immediate family.

❑ The executor will meet with a lawyer to ensure that he or she is administering the estate according to the will's instructions. The lawyer can give advice on any potential legal issues. The executor will be responsible for paying all probate fees, legal, accounting or other fees associated with the executor's duties. "Probate" is the legal process whereby a will is declared valid and the authority of the executor is confirmed. Therefore besides confirming the extent of the estate, probate also serves to protect the executor.

❑ The executor will work with the next of kin, family members, and possibly former family members, as well as business partners and potential creditors.

❑ The executor must make an inventory of all the deceased's personal belongings, and business assets, as well as pull together all the documents in order to wind-down his or her affairs. The executor should quickly get in touch with the deceased's financial advisor.

❑ The executor must contact all insurance companies (life, health, home, car, business), and employers or former employers. He or she must advise the federal government with respect to benefits, i.e. CPP & OAS, and the provincial government with respect to health coverage. Outstanding debts will need to be paid, banks advised, leases broken, subscriptions stopped, mail re-directed etc.

❑ Assets will need to be gathered, managed, sold or transferred, including investment, business and real estate assets, as per the will's direction.

❑ The executor will determine the value of the estate after paying all liabilities including taxes. There can be more than one tax return which must be filed when a person dies, so the executor will probably choose to work with a professional tax preparer or an accountant. The executor will want to obtain formal clearance from the Canada Customs & Revenue Agency (CCRA) before estate distributions are made to the heirs.

❑ The executor will meet with the beneficiaries and arrange for the distribution of outstanding assets or for the residual of the estate.

"As there were no banks in Roman times, when gold coinage came in, money would be buried in a pot, and if the man should die without telling where his money was, it might stay there until turned up by accident."

C. T. Currelly, *I Brought the Ages Home*

I hope this chapter has been informative and not too burdensome to read. And I hope it has inspired you to take action for the responsibility of your affairs. If you haven't done anything until this point with respect to insurance and beneficiaries, wills and powers of attorney, then you still have done "estate planning" it's just that it has been inadequate and expensive estate planning. And nobody is going to thank you for that.

Like the other aspects of financial planning, estate planning is a continual process and you will alter your plans to fit your circumstances. You should review your will and powers of attorney every few years or more frequently if there has been a life event in your immediate family, such as a wedding, birth, death or divorce. You may not need to have your whole will re-written, just a small change made, and this is where your lawyer's advise is valuable.

I cannot stress enough the importance of having updated, professionally prepared documents. Marc and I lost a wedding guest to cancer three weeks before our marriage. She was 41, with a 4 year old daughter and a husband. Another guest died six weeks after our wedding of an aneurysm. He was 57. You can imagine how hard it was for us to attend the funerals of our wedding guests. We do not know where on the spectrum our life span will fall. But we can be prepared to share in the joy and the sadness, knowing we will experience both along the way. Nobody goes through life untouched and unaffected by the lives of others. Our preparations help to make the journey easier. Estate planning is a very unselfish act.

> **"Life does not cease to be funny when people die anymore than it ceases to be serious when people laugh."**
> George Bernard Shaw, playwright

Chapter Twenty

Carey B. & Roberta B.

Carey and Roberta are both in their early forties. The three of us were childhood friends. Although we remained in touch on and off through the years, this interview was the first time we had taken the time to be together, just the three of us, in probably thirty years.

Carey is divorced with two daughters and works in conference sales for a resort. Roberta is married with two daughters and is a gemologist.

I'm hoping one day, you will give this book to your girls. What would you want your girls to know?

R: Never spend more than you have. And never spend as much as you make.

Okay, end of book, nothing more needs to be said. Is that something you learned the hard way?

R: Well, when I was in university and was doing co-op terms, I knew whatever I made had to last me through the next term at school. At that point I could only spend at maximum, half of what I was making. Of course later things changed when I got married and had kids.

C: A long time ago I read *The Wealthy Barber*. *The Wealthy Barber* gives an incredible piece of advice, and if I wanted my girls to do something, I would like them to start very soon putting away 10%. Whatever they're making on a summer job, put 10% of it away. Ten percent is so small and if you start saving at 18 ...

R: Or at 8. My girls get an allowance every week. They get half their age in dollars. So my oldest gets $5 a week, and of that she's expected to give a little bit to the church and some of it has to go into her long terms savings. We kept the "long term savings" in a jar on the counter for the longest time and now we've got it in a bank account. And my girls both have almost $200 in that account. It's not a lot of money, but it's a lot of money to them and they call it their "house fund" – they're planning to buy their houses with this.

C: And I read in another book, you should have part of the kids' allowance go back into a savings program, but also add the interest. Take pennies or dimes to represent interest and add them to the jar so the kids can see their savings build – you make your own interest in the jar. So if they're putting a dollar a week in the jar, you say OK 10% of that is a dime and every week you add a dime. But you keep track, so when the jar has $22 dollars in it from all the dimes, then you take 10% of that and put it in. The kids see the interest compounding. Unfortunately, it's too late for me because now my girls just want to spend.

Carey, as young teenagers what perceptions of money do you think your kids have.

C: I don't think they have a good perception of money, and as a single parent I'm constantly struggling.

As adults, its rare that a couple has the exact same style of managing money, but we somehow have to give our kids a message and decide on what that is. It's much harder in a divorced relationship.

C: Definitely. And I do not live with the comfort of a double income.

R: You can get into the situation where one parent is essentially trying to buy the affections of the kids from the other parent.

Money is like everything else, in that kids try to figure out how this all works in the big scheme of things. And they get mixed messages, between media, parents and their cohorts.

R: My older daughter will try and ask my younger daughter, Alina, for money to buy a toy or whatever. I predict Alina will always have enough money because she doesn't spend it. Alina will be very careful about how she spends her money.

C: Jessica is the same. Sarah spends it all, Jess hoards it all. Here's an example that happened in my family and I'll never forget it. A couple of years ago my Dad and Mom and I met my brother and his fiancée in a nice restaurant in downtown Toronto to celebrate their engagement. As we were leaving the restaurant, Dad looks at his watch and he says "Oh, if I run I'll save a dollar in the parking place." He says "Mary & Carey you wait outside and I'll pick you up." And he *ran*. I looked at my Mom and I said "I can't believe what I'm seeing. I can't believe it."

Do you think its true what they say about wealthy people, they are wealthy because they value every dollar?

C: They do things like that, absolutely. And Mom said to me "Carey, that's why he's got the loonies in his pocket." I said, "I guess that's why I never do and I never will because I'd be walking slowly." I never would have run, never. That's how ingrained it is in my Dad, and he tried his very best to teach us. As a matter of fact I thought my parents' allowance plan was pretty good. I think when I was about 12 or 13 he asked us kids for a budget. I don't know if you remember this.

R: That happened to me too.

C: And we said "A budget? What's that?" So my Dad explained that he wanted us to categorize where we spent money. And "how much do you spend a year on clothes to go to school? Because we are going to give you this much money." "How much do you need for going to the movies? How much do you need for gas for the car?" I remember getting to age 16 and thinking how far can I push this. My sister said to me, "How much do we need for beer money?"

What do you categorize that under?

C & R: Entertainment, of course.

C: So he would give us the money up front every year. It had to last a year.

R: Mine had to last six months.

C: I think it ended up getting to be about $1,500.

R: Oh you were in gravy. I had $300 bucks to last me six months.

C: Oh God, no. But we had a whole list of things that $1,500 had to buy.

R: My $300 had to cover clothes, music, entertainment, shampoo, toothpaste, tampons.

C: Tampons! Oh yeah, I guess I was lucky then. (*Lots of laughter.*)

I think you are both going to have a discussion with your parents when you see them next.

R: That was my grandfather, who is dead now. But my Mom felt so sorry for me that every once in a while I would come home and there would be new underwear on my bed she'd bought for me because mine was getting so ratty.

I remember you would sew your own underwear.

R: Well, yes. I couldn't buy it. I didn't have any money!

I always admired you for that.

C: Wow.

R: This started when I was 14. My grandfather gave me $300 to last me six months and I had to do a budget. And he expected 10% to go to the church, which was a little bit of a laugh considering I didn't have a church at the time. But it kept Grandpa happy and that was my slush fund.

C: Perfect.

R: I accounted for everything down to the penny. It started on my birthday. Six months later, so in February, I had to produce the accounting of the previous $300 and the budget for the next $300, before I'd get it.

C: See, I never had to do all that. I didn't have to be accountable but I probably should have. I always remember the message was extremely clear: if this isn't enough, get a job. And that's what I did, because it wasn't enough.

R: Well mine wasn't enough either. It's interesting, so you modified your budget on the income side. I modified mine on the expense side by cutting back the expenses.

And by sewing your own underwear.

C: I probably would have benefited by hanging-out with you a bit more Roberta.

Carey's still just learning there's an expense side to the equation.

C: Oh God!

R: Well it's interesting because now I'm a stay at home mom. How do I handle our finances? I have to modify the expense side.

Carey, as a single mom what have you had to learn?

C: I've learned that if I didn't have my Mom & Dad I'd be living in subsidized housing on welfare, plus working. I'd be doing both.

You'd be the working poor?

C: Yes. I work in the hospitality industry which doesn't pay high wages to begin with. I live outside of a city, so again the income level drops. Yes, the cost of living as far as housing and real estate taxes goes is less, but food and clothing, gas and insurance costs are all the same. My Mom & Dad have been incredible. I'm so grateful and appreciative and it bothers me that my kids aren't as grateful and appreciative, but they're being coached from the other side. Unfortunately, my poor kids are getting a lot of mixed messages and they'll have to sort them out.

Did both of you inherit money from grandparents?

C: I did.
R: Well, no.

I'm not asking to be nosey. I'm interested on your thoughts on inherited money.

R: I was just thinking we should probably have a big section on inherited money.
C: I did inherit money. It's definitely good, but something which I recognize, which has happened to me, is that now there is a comfort zone.

Because of the money?

C: Yes.

R: Because you do not have to plan for your retirement quite as much.

C: It's true, and my sister keeps reminding me that there will be more. And I never think about that. She thinks our parents won't need everything they've got.

The counseling I try to give my clients is don't bank on inherited money. We are all living longer, and you don't know what your parents' medical care expenses will be when they are in their nineties.

C: Exactly, Heather. I agree with you 100%.

R: You can't count on an inheritance.

I also find there's a difference between American thinking and Canadian thinking. Americans believe in passing money down through the generations. Whereas Canadians are more likely to say, "No, I had to work for it, so my kids are going to have to work for it." I feel there is a role for inherited money, it depends on the individual family and how that money is passed down.

R: It's interesting to talk about this. When my Mom's parents died she received an inheritance. It wasn't an outrageous amount but she went out and invested it and has done extremely well. She now uses her little personal fortune to do renovations on the house without any arguments or discussions with my father. She spends her money as she jolly well pleases.

Then my father's father died about seven and half years ago and his estate was split. Half went to his wife and the other half was divested to his three kids. Now neither my father

213

nor his two sisters required any extra income. So my dad set up trusts for his children [the grandchildren]. Now we would have thought, "Give it over. You don't need it. Hand it on down now, I could use it." But no, he set up a trust and there's a certain flow-through for my children. I don't get it, but it comes through in-trust for my kids. It's essentially the same effect. The money comes directly into my children's bank accounts every month, most of which is used to fund an insurance policy for each of them. That leaves a small residual which I use to buy things like shoes, but it doesn't come close to covering expenses such as tutoring, orthodontics, speech therapy. It makes me think "Okay Dad, cough up some more inheritance now when it's useful."

I come from a very long line of long-lived people. There's no way I'm going to get any direct inheritance until I'm well into my retirement. My grandmother is in her nineties and could live for another 10 years, and my husband would like to retire in another 5 to 6 years. We won't have an inheritance when my husband retires, not from his Mom either, who is thinking of doing some intergenerational planning too.

So neither of you came into a lump sum of money, which taught you quickly about handling it?

C: I did. I got a lump sum of money when my aunt died although it came from my grandparents. It didn't teach me anything, but it gave me a buffer zone. In a way it's been a negative in my mind, because I got into a pattern of spending more because I knew that lump sum of money was there. It's weird because a year or so ago I was living paycheque to paycheque – I did not have an extra dime. I was getting fed up, and my boyfriend said to me "You've got that money, Carey go to your investment guy and ask him for a couple of hundred dollars a month, for the summer at least so you have money to do things with the kids." I thought that was a good idea and I went and did that. Well that "for the summer" plan lasted a year and a bit, so I phoned my money guy and I said "I think I need to stop that now." He said, "Are you sure?" And I said, "Yes I'm sure." I'm glad I did because it was silly, at one point I was paying $30 a month into a fund but taking $200 a month out.

Anyway, I'm back to putting money in and not taking money out, but at the same time I'm being supplemented by my parents – God love them. Because I'd still be living paycheque to paycheque without their help. It's impossible for me to live without a line of credit. I would explain it to my parents. My Dad's great, he always asks how's it going? "Not so good Dad" I'd reply. He'd say, "Why, what's going on?" I'd say "the bottom line, do you want to know the bottom line?" He'd say yup. "I spend more money than I make. Bottom line."

And part of this situation, which I realize and I've thought about, is that I was raised in a higher lifestyle than I now have on my own. I got used to that lifestyle, and to obliterate it is very hard. It's easier to be raised in a lifestyle with less and remain used to that, to stick with that. It's very difficult to pretty much have had everything you needed and most of the things you wanted, and all of a sudden to have not enough so that you're scrimping. It's really tough.

And if your family and friends are still in that lifestyle and you want to be a part of their lives …

C: Exactly.
R: You do need to be able to pull back.
C: I agree and I do.
R: I think it is very important to be able to live within your means. I know what you mean about having a certain lifestyle. Look at how my parents live, they spend half their

time in Tucson, and look at all the rest that they have. But then you look at how my two sisters, my brother and I have attacked it. I think my brother is the only one who has a little bit of trouble living within his means. If he sees a toy out there he'll go and buy it – he's always got to have the fastest computer, the most up-to-date palm pilot, the best car. I can't envision having that level of toys and that level of spending on our income. We do just fine on one income, but I think one of the reasons we do just fine and live in such a nice house is because I am *very* careful. If I see that cash flow is beginning to get tight, I pull back. I'll say to the kids, "We're not buying cookies. If you want cookies, you make cookies. I'm not spending $4 on a box of cookies. No way." So we haven't had cookies in the house for weeks! The kids are too lazy to make them and I'm not going to buy them.

C: That's something I should add to the discussion, that in growing up, somehow I never properly learned how to make a budget, follow it and keep it. I know it's a simple thing and maybe it means taking 3 hours a month to list everything that you've spent and everything that comes in, and balance the difference. Probably that's my biggest downfall.
R: There is an easier way of doing it. It's not nearly as much work.
C: Well that's what I need to learn. I don't take the 3 hours a month. I have a pile this high of "Things To Be Filed."
R: You have a computer – do you have Quicken? Do you have a personal financial management system? Use Quicken. It's brilliant. It's easy to use. I keep track of our bank account, in fact I even have the automatic download from the bank so I know everyday what my bank balance is, and I download it into Quicken and reconcile all the transactions. I also use it to keep track of the credit cards. I easily pay for the fees on the credit cards by the mistakes that I find, because I save every single chit and it gets added into Quicken. And I use the categories, and the budgeting.

So for the month it will say you've already spent this month's budget on internet access, or you've spent this month's budget on …

C: But you're entering that in.

R: I am.

C: How long does it take you?

R: I did it yesterday morning – it took me two hours for the whole month of August.

C: So it is two hours a month?

R: Yeah, it's nothing.

C: It isn't.

I think you have to want to do it too.

C: I want to do it.

It's sort of like looking after your health, there comes a point when you want to start making the changes.

C: I want to start.

R: This week I went up to my Mom's and taught her how to use Quicken. I can show it to you Carey.

C: I'd love you to show it to me.

R: The biggest trick with budgeting is knowing beforehand how much money you have to spend. And then to stop. That's the trick, you stop spending once you've reached your budget. You say to yourself, it's the 19th of the month, I've spent my budget on booze, so that's it. No more wine for me for the rest of the month! (*Laughter.*)

Advice for your daughters – I think number one for you both was to manage money?

C: Absolutely.

R: Make a budget.

C: Follow the budget, and the 10% savings rule. And start when you're young.

If you have your kids putting aside 10% for the long-term, what do they think long-term is? Is it "when I'm an adult" or is it for a goal which is a year or two down the road?

C: Long-term is for retirement.
R: It's for forever.
C: Start at 17 years of age putting 10% aside for when you want to retire. If you start when you're 17 you can retire at 55 much more easily.
R: You cannot do the 10% rule unless you can figure out the budgeting.
C: You're right.
R: As you were saying, if you are in a negative cash flow situation where you're spending more than you have, you cannot do the 10% rule because you're at negative 15%.
C: You're exactly right.

C: Something else I'd like my girls to know, I wished I'd started some kind of insurance plan for them when they were one year old. Maybe when they are young mother's they can start something for their children as soon as they are born, so that when their kids are 18 or 20 they'll have an asset to use to send them to university.

You're referring to a Universal Life policy and there are interesting things you can do with insurance. Life insurance can be very simple or you can have a policy with all sorts of bells & whistles. You can get overwhelmed by the options or by the person who's trying to sell you a particular policy. However, it's worth doing your research because insurance does give you some interesting options.

R: The problem with a lot of financial products is you get yourself into a situation where you really need to trust your financial advisor. Between Alex, myself and the girls, we have five investment accounts and I haven't a clue as to what all of these mutual funds are in the accounts.

C: With mutual funds you have to look at your investment as long-term. If you look at them as short-term you'll drive yourself insane.

R: Yes, you will. On Thursday I was in with my current investment advisor and he was saying, "These funds have done very poorly … this particular fund has a new manager and I don't like his style …" I said, "Look Bob, I have no clue. Why are you asking my advice?"

C: It's so true. You have to trust the person.

It can be frightening, the level of trust you need to have.

C: It is. My advisor never calls me. I don't like that, and it's not that I don't trust him.   I do, I trust his advice, I trust his opinion, but I'm starting to question him now.

You know you just need to drop him an email or a voice message saying "George, I trust you but I need to hear from you more often." Because, the other thing to remember is, that different clients have totally different expectations.

C: You're right.

Some of my clients need to hear from me often, and in fact some of my clients don't want to. As an advisor you want to stay in contact with your clients but you don't want them to think you're hassling them to give you money every time you call. But I think you've raised a really good point. At the end of the day it's your money.

C: Yes.

So you have a right to say these are my expectations, including expectations of return. If you are saying to your advisor I'm expecting a 20% rate of return every year, your advisor will advise you otherwise. But you need to make your expectations known; what kind of contact you want and when. And you know what? It may change for you. At first you may have been fine with the level of contact, but now you know a little bit more, or for whatever reason, you may want more contact and you have a right to say that. Your advisor needs to know that.

R: I was a little annoyed with the previous guy we were dealing with because I got the feeling that we were getting a canned set of goods. We would go down to see him, we'd chat about fishing, and it was almost as though that was the reason we were there.
C: He wasn't taking your financial needs seriously?
R: No, he was doing the standard and there was no effort to be creative. So when we came here it took us the better part of a year for me to find somebody that I liked.

Meanwhile, we all know that life continues to "happen." And planning is why you need to go back and review what you've done. Is it still right for you? Are you still comfortable with your planning?

C: My Dad has an estate planner who is my age, and apparently this guy is brilliant. My sister and her husband have gone to see him. My parents love him and my brother calls him the prodigal son.
R: Well, I tell you Carey, there's something to be said for dealing with somebody who knows your entire family.
C: That's what I'm starting to think. This guy knows my family, why am I not using this guy?
R: Exactly, he'll know the whole picture.

C: I am going to set-up a meeting. I want to look at my overall picture with some advice, you know, the whole story.
R: Sometimes it's a full-time job just to keep track of all your financial stuff.
C: It's tough.

It's becoming like that, isn't it? You remember Grandma Duncan? Well I think of her retiring on saved grocery money, and ...

C: Saved grocery money?

Yes, her husband gave her money for the groceries and she didn't spend it all. But you know what, it didn't last through her retirement.

R: Saved grocery money is not much money.

No, but that's what it was like a few generations ago.

C: There are women going through the same thing now.
R: Sure.
C: Trust me, there are lots of women who are.
R: Yes, and there is this whole other issue when you are talking about finances: how do you organize your finances? When Alex and I got married, we made the decision "one family, one name, one bank account." So we don't have his money and her money we have "our money." If any thing were ever to fall out between Alex and I, we'd have a hell of a time. Either that, or it would be dead easy: 50/50. But I know that my parents do things completely differently. They are shocked and amazed that Alex and I share the same bank account, to them it's like sharing a toothbrush.
(*Lots of laughter.*)

C: I love it.

R: I couldn't imagine doing it any other way. Because I do not have any income, if we had separate bank accounts I would feel always that I had to be asking for money. I would hate that. I would absolutely hate it.

C: It's interesting that you bring this up, because in my relationship with my ex-husband we had one bank account. It was similar to your one bank account, but believe me it wasn't organized. It was loosey-goosey. But he always stressed that it had to be one account. "You don't have your money and I have my money. It's all one piece of the pie." Which was fine. But now I'm contemplating things with my boyfriend Jim because he and I are going to move in together. I haven't discussed this actual subject with him and I'm thinking how are we going to do it? I've pretty much decided. I'm sure it's going to be two separate accounts, because that's the way he's always lived so how could I say to him "Oh well it's all one big pie?" You know what I mean?

I don't think there's a clear-cut answer for that. I think you have to work out what's best for you. But also, I think you're right Roberta, you do have to keep in mind that something could happen to your relationship. I'm not saying you in particular, I'm saying we as women need to think, okay what if something happened? What if my husband was unfaithful and I wanted to leave the relationship?

C: Do you not have a pre-nuptial agreement?

No we don't, but we do have separate banking.

C: See, I'm getting a pre-nup.
R: I didn't get a pre-nup.
C: I didn't either but I'll tell you because of what I've gone through, and what I know about society and what the world is like, I would never jeopardize …
R: Well you are in a totally different situation at this point.

C: Oh, I am. I've now got financial security and some independence for myself and my kids and I could never jeopardize that.

R: Because your kids are not Jim's kids.

C: That's right.

R: And you're going to get in a situation where you'll inherit some money and you're going to want that to flow through to your children.

C: Right.

R: You wouldn't necessarily want Jim to receive your inheritance.

C: Exactly. Well he's going to have an inheritance too. So why would he want that money to go to my kids?

R: Yeah. When Alex and I came together we both brought in essentially the same amount of money. We both had a house; when we added it up it we were within $5,000 of each other. So it made sense to say, "Okay that's our starting point." I have kept meticulous records of all of our finances since we were married. I know exactly where the money has gone, on everything.

C: That's fabulous. I envy you for that.

R: It's not hard.

C: Quicken?

Well once you get a system in place that works for you, it's just a question of updating it or maintaining it.

R: So if for any chance things were to go sour, I certainly have the records. When Ian and I were together, we had separate bank accounts. Again, I ran the household. We weren't married although we were common-law. And so I suppose after having lived together for 8 years, if either of us had wanted to be nasty at our break-up, we could have been. We weren't. But the way I ran it at that time, I would just say to Ian, I need so much money for your portion of the household expenses and he would give it to me. He never questioned my accounting of it. But I don't know whether I would want to be in a situation like that again. I know friends of mine who have two incomes in a household, and they alternate who pays the bills.

C: Monthly?

R: Yes. Monthly or yearly.

C: That's weird, isn't it?

R: So this year he pays the mortgage and she pays the gas, then next year she pays the mortgage and he pays the gas.

That's the first time I've ever heard of that arrangement, but I think well if it works for them, that's good.

R: I think everybody has to come up with their own thing. I think when you're running one household it's very difficult unless you keep meticulous records, to make sure things are always fair.

Yesterday, we got into a great discussion talking about health issues. We have no problem talking about health or vitamins or diets or exercise or ...

C: Or booze.

R: I don't think we have any problem talking about money either.

Well that was going to be my question. Have you found this conversation to be comfortable and have you found it informative?

R: Sure.

Have you found it interesting?

C: Absolutely. Both.

Trust is a key issue, but I think if you are with women you trust, it is okay to talk about money and finances and investments.

R: Yes, but Heather, we've got here sitting at this table three of the oldest friends. If the three of us can't trust each other, down to our very bones and with our life-blood, then we can trust nobody. And I'm not sure whether any of us would have this level of comfort with somebody we knew casually.
C: Or even if we'd only known them for ten years.

The relationship has to be there first. Now, let's say we live to 90 and we are retired for 30 years. We're all living longer, and our living costs are going to triple during that time.

R: Yes.

So I think it's worth saying to each other - for me to be able to say, "I care about you and your health. Also, I care about you and your finances."

R: You bring up a good point Heather, because in the past year we had a nice woman from one of the banks come and sit in our living room and she put together one of those retirement forecasts. You know you plug all your numbers into the computer and it basically tells you whether or not you can hope to retire when you want to. Which means you have to save more money than you ever dreamed possible, and you're not going to have enough. And when I looked at her final analysis she had me living in poverty.
C: That's unacceptable.
R: I know. She said, "Well, you're only going to need 40% of your current income." I'm not going to need 40% of my current income. I'm going to need 150% of my current income, at least. Because when we are all retired, we're going to be playing, right?

225

C: Exactly.

R: That an early but poor retirement is a good retirement is a complete fallacy. I'm going to live a long time, I want to be in good health – with a little luck, and I don't want to be poor. I want to have gobs of money so I can travel the world, and play, and do whatever I want.

For a lot of people that is the cost of the first half of their retirement: fulfilling their dreams, doing the things they want to do. Then the cost of the second half of their retirement could be medical needs. That's why as women, the more we look after our health now, the less it's going to cost us in real, money/dollar terms down the road.

R: Sure, because hiring private nurses is expensive.

C: Well, I'm certainly very attuned to and aware of taking care of myself nutritionally.

I'm just starting.

C: Heather, something I've seen with you, and I've come to know over the past years regarding health, is that there is a serious balance between body, mind and soul.

R: Yes, absolutely. And when you're happy, you're healthy.

And when you're relaxed, you're healthy.

C: You have to consciously work on all three. One of the things that I work on in my life is finding the balance between work and play, between health and un-health.

Well, Ninka's how old now?

R: She's ten.

Because I remember it was with Ninka that you asked certain women to send her a godmother wish.

C & R: Oh, yeah.

I remember my wish for her, and I didn't have to think about it, it was balance. That's what I wished for Ninka, balance in her life.

C: I wonder what I sent? *(Laughter)* I can't remember. Ten years ago I don't think I was doing so well. Things were not good then.

Absolutely balance.

C: It's a key. And balance in your finances too.

I know exactly the projections and illustrations the woman from the bank did. I do them for clients too and I warn them. I think they're good to do but I say "Look it's not going to be fun, it's like standing in front of the mirror naked. Okay? But we'll see where we want to do some work." I warn them it's a depressing exercise to go through.

R: One of the credo's for living is: why ask a question if you don't know what you're going to do with the answer. And this is one of those things. You know that in order to retire as well as you want, you're going to have to save more than you think you can, for longer than you think you want to, in order to have not quite as much money as you're going to need when you retire.

I think I'll quote you on that. If I can just follow along one more time.

C & R: Well you've got it on tape!

C: Rewind, rewind, forward, play, rewind, forward, play ...

Okay, now I get it, now I get it. (More laughter.)

R: We've got this long painful procedure of plugging numbers into a computer program that's going to end up ...

That's it: it just tells you where we need to do some work. That's what it tells you.

R: Well you're going to need to save more money for longer than you thought ...

Than you actually bring in. You have to save more money than you actually earn. Okay. We can do that!

C: Heather will be at the computer for weeks transcribing this one.

No, I find this fascinating. There's so much we can learn from one another, and some messages need to be reinforced. We're not crazy. We do have heads on our shoulders. It is an issue of trust. It is our money. We do need to find things out. It is more complicated than it used to be. If you're going to live into your nineties you can't brush-off, in the market world that we live in, the responsibility of managing your finances.

R: I personally am not interested in planning for a retirement that is poor and short.
C: No.
R: I want to plan for a retirement that is going to be long, healthy and fun!

About the author

Heather Duncan is a Certified Financial Planner who has been struck by people's ability to adapt to change. She works with one of Canada's largest financial services companies, providing advice to individual clients. Prior to becoming a CFP, she spent a number of years in the consulting and human resources field, and even worked as a flight attendant.

Heather has known many people from different backgrounds. Her concern is fueled by professional and personal experience. Heather speaks passionately on the topic of planning for our old age. She cares about her clients and her audience, and wants each person to benefit from a dignified standard of living throughout their entire lives.

Heather can be reached at:

www.heatherduncan.ca

(613) 236-1733
1-866-821-0233

or

Heather Duncan, CFP
P.O. Box 4704
Station "E"
Ottawa, ON   K1S 5H8
Canada